T0070104

FROM NOW UNTIL THEN

An Eschatological Review of End Time Issues

DR. BILLY LINDSEY

WESTBOW
PRESS®
A DIVISION OF THOMAS NELSON
& ZONDERVAN

Scripture taken from the King James Version of the Bible.

WestBow Press books may be ordered through booksellers or by contacting:

WestBow Press
A Division of Thomas Nelson & Zondervan
1663 Liberty Drive
Bloomington, IN 47403
www.westbowpress.com
1 (866) 928-1240

Because of the dynamic nature of the Internet, any web addresses or links contained in this book may have changed since publication and may no longer be valid. The views expressed in this work are solely those of the author and do not necessarily reflect the views of the publisher, and the publisher hereby disclaims any responsibility for them.

Any people depicted in stock imagery provided by Thinkstock are models, and such images are being used for illustrative purposes only. Certain stock imagery © Thinkstock.

ISBN: 978-1-5127-3309-9 (sc)
ISBN: 978-1-5127-3311-2 (hc)
ISBN: 978-1-5127-3310-5 (e)

Library of Congress Control Number: 2016903429

Print information available on the last page.

WestBow Press rev. date: 03/11/2016

TABLE OF CONTENTS

TABLES

ILLUSTRATIONS

ACKNOWLEDGEMENTS

I did not know, when I started toying with the thought of writing this book, that so many people would be required in the completion of such a project. First of all, my wife, son, and daughter. I must also include my daughter-in-law and son-in-law. Thanks to both of you for "fitting like a glove" into our family. A tremendous thank you goes to my wife. She will never know the great help she was to me. She is gifted at spelling and also has an uncanny ability to remember and recall scripture. When I would get down, she was so good at lifting me up again. Her encouragement was always clothed with love, care, and concern. I have read many acknowledgements by other writers, and they would always say, "I could not have written this book had it not been for the help of my wife." I now know what they were talking about. So I dedicate this effort to my family, especially my wife.

There are so many others that have been so helpful in this writing. Phil Russell, who is deep in the scripture, especially in prophecy. Phil is good with his quick knowledge of the scripture. Thanks to John Powell, Mike O'Brian, Ken Warnke, Stephen Whitmon, Neal Narmore, Jim Lumpkin, Roger Moore, Mickey Elkins, and others who meet at our Saturday morning prophecy meetings. I am glad all of you came my way.

I am so grateful to my Wednesday night prophecy class that I have been teaching for over ten years. Your encouragement and prayers have meant so much to me. I especially thank you for your faithfulness.

And as they say, last but not least is Carla Horton. I do not believe a book could be written if the writer did not have someone like a Carla Horton. She was the editor, the typist, and any question that anyone had would wind up on Carla's desk. Carla has had her feet to the fire many times before. She served in this position for the Muscle Shoals School System which required more expertise than typing a book. Carla, I want to thank you for managing this book. You did a great job.

Dennis you will never know how much you have meant to the completion of this book. I can't say enough how much I appreciate your work and your great positive attitude toward the completion of this book. Thank you Dennis.

There is a song that I love so dearly. Its title is "Jesus, I Love You." I have listened to that song so many times. That is the way I feel right now. Jesus, I love you. Every time I hear this song, the tears of joy and love in my eyes won't let me read or write. I just have to stop and be blessed. So, thank you, Jesus, for letting me take this trip, **From Now Until Then**, I have been truly blessed.

Chapter 1

THE 70TH WEEK OF DANIEL

To me, this is some of the most astounding prophecy in the entire Bible. This prophecy was delivered to Daniel by Gabriel. It gives us the chronology of Israel's future history. Much of this prophecy has already been fulfilled. Because of this fulfillment, we can interpret this prophecy literally. To interpret this prophecy literally makes it actually seem possible and simple to understand. What makes this prophecy so amazing is to realize that only an omniscient God could foretell the events over 500 years in advance of the day the Messiah would ride into Jerusalem and declare himself as the "Prince" of Israel as we will see later.

In Leviticus 24:3-4, we find the following instructions:

For six years thou shall sow thy field, and six years thou shall prune thy vineyard, and gather in the fruit thereof; but in the seventh year shall be a Sabbath of rest unto the land, a Sabbath for the Lord: thou shall neither sow thy field, nor prune thy vineyard.

The Jews were allowed to plow, work, and sow their land for "six years." But the seventh year, the land was to lay fallow. They were allowed to plow the land but were not allowed to sow the land. The seventh year was a year to be a solemn "Sabbath of rest unto the land." The Jews violated the divine law of the sabbatic year. They violated this law for 70 years. Their penalty for violating this divine law would

1

be 70 years of captivity. That would be 70 sabbatic years or a total of 490 years (seven times seventy equals 490 years). Here, Daniel has been reading Jeremiah about "years," "seventy years." Because of the preaching and writing of Jeremiah, Daniel knew the captivity would last for 70 years. To fulfill the word of the Lord by the mouth of Jeremiah, until the land had enjoyed her sabbaths: for as long as she lay desolate she kept sabbath, to fulfill three score and ten years" (2 Chronicles 36:21). For clarification purposes, the following illustrations will help you to understand the difficult prophecy given to Daniel. Once this becomes clear in your mind, you will see the awesome power of God in delivering the 70 weeks of years prophecy to Daniel. [1]

Illustration I
1 Week	=	7 years
70 Weeks	=	490 years

70 Weeks is divided into three periods:
7 Weeks	(49 years)		
62 Weeks	(434 years)		
1 Week	(7 years)	=	490 years

Illustration II

This shows how the 70 Weeks of Years are divided into the three parts:

7 Weeks + 62 Weeks + 1 Week	=	70 Weeks
7 Weeks of Years	=	49 Years
62 Weeks of Years	=	434 Years

(A total of 69 Weeks of Years makes 483 years)

1 Week (the last)	=	7 Years

(A total of 70 Weeks of Years makes 490 years)

The last week of years is also divided into two halves of 3 ½ years each.

Until the appearing of the Messiah as Prince, 7 + 62 = 69 Weeks of Years will pass.

Two princes are mentioned: one is the Messiah Prince and the other is a future prince, "the prince that shall come, "which refers to the antichrist world ruler.[2]

These seventy sevens are for Israel. We need to know that the end of the seventy sevens and the Times of the Gentiles will both end at the same time. This will be at the second coming of Jesus Christ. Sixty-nine weeks of those seventy weeks have already been fulfilled. Only one week remains to be fulfilled. God stopped the time clock at Pentecost. He will start the time clock again with the signing of the peace covenant between the antichrist and Israel. With the starting of that time clock, God will start the last week of the seventy weeks. At the end of this week, Jesus Christ will come back to this earth to set up His millennial kingdom. The Church, His Bride, will be with Him.

Six things must be accomplished by the end of the 490 years (Daniel 9:24):

(1) *To finish the transgression.* This is in reference to the transgression of Israel. The Jews have still not accepted Jesus Christ as their Messiah, and they will not until the end of the last week of the "seventy weeks" (Hosea 6:1-3). In these verses, you will hear the voice of the remnant in the last days.

   ○ Come and let us return unto the Lord: for he hath torn and he will heal us; he hath smitten and he will build us up.
   ○ After two days will he revive us: in the third day, he will raise us up and we shall live in his sight.
   ○ Then shall we know, if we follow on to know the Lord, his going forth is prepared as the morning; and he shall come unto us as the rain, as the latter and former rain unto the earth.

Look at bullet two above. For two days before He returns, this remnant will plead with Jesus Christ to redeem them. They now realize that He is the Messiah. He is their Messiah. And in the third day He will raise them up and they shall live in His sight.

In the third bullet, He is telling them that He is going to come unto them. We are told in the scriptures that He is going to save Israel. In these verses, He is going to do just that. In that last "week" we are told God says, "And I will pour upon the house of David, and upon the inhabitants of Jerusalem, the spirit of grace and of supplications: and they shall look upon me whom they have pierced, and they shall mourn for him, as one mourneth for his only son...." (Zachariah 12:10). The spirit is poured out on this delivered remnant and Jesus Christ is revealed to them.

(2) *To make an end of sins.* "The national sins of Israel will come to an end at the end of the second coming of Christ." [3] The people in Israel are sinners. The nation of Israel are sinners. As a nation, Israel has made major mistakes but so have all other nations including America.

(3) *To make reconciliation for iniquity.* The death of Jesus Christ on the cross has provided redemption for both the Jews and Gentiles. Thank God for the resurrection of Jesus Christ and He lives today. His plea of "whosoever will" is for ALL.

(4) *And to bring in everlasting righteousness.* This has reference to the return of Christ at the end of the 490 years to establish His kingdom. Look at the words *everlasting righteousness*. No one will enter the millennium who is not saved. Yes, there will be sin during the 1,000 years. The sheep who enter will be saved but they will still be in their natural bodies. There will be rebellion by their offspring even to the point they will make war against Jesus Christ. Satan will try to defeat Jesus but he will fail and that will be the end of Satan.

(5) *To seal up the vision of prophecy.* This indicates that all prophecy will be fulfilled. The subject of the Seventy Sevens is the final fulfillment of all prophecy. To seal up means to shut up prophecy. This part of God's plan is fulfilled. The purpose of all prophecy

will end at the second coming of the messiah. Prophets could not see beyond the messianic kingdom. [4]

(6) *To anoint the most holy place.* This refers to the anointing of a place and not a person. It refers to the most holy place in the temple. And that to the fourth temple or the temple of the messianic kingdom which will be built by the Lord himself. This anointing will be part of the program of Seventy Sevens. [5]

Daniel 9:25-27 is the starting point for the period of 490 years for Israel to get her act together. Nehemiah 2:1-8 reinforces the scripture referenced in Daniel as the 490 year starting point. The decree of Artaxerxes in the 20th year of his reign meets the requirements of Daniel 9:25. The commandment was given to rebuild the city of Jerusalem including the rebuilding of its walls. This command was issued in the month of Nisan 445 B.C. Artaxerxes came into power in 465 B.C. So he was in his 20th year of rule when the command was issued. This takes us to 445 B.C. (465-20 = 445 B.C.). The task of rebuilding the wall and the city of Jerusalem had to be completed in seven weeks or 49 years. It was completed right on schedule. This also completes the first week of the 70 weeks leaving 69 weeks. Sixty-two weeks, which is 434 years, brings us to the Messiah. Jesus Christ will be crucified after seven weeks (49 years) and sixty-two weeks (434 years) for a total of sixty-nine weeks or 483 years. We know that the last week of seventy weeks is the tribulation week. If you take the 483 years (69 x7 = 483) and multiply it by the Jewish method of measuring time, which is 360 days in a year, that totals 173,880 days. From the date that Nehemiah said "you may go ahead and rebuild your wall and Jerusalem (March 14, 445 B.C.) to the day Jesus Christ rode into Jerusalem on the back of a donkey (April 6, 32 A.D.) is exactly 173,880 days. Now, how could you believe this prophecy is not right on? This is the most exciting, soul rendering, amazing prophecy given by Daniel over 500 years before it happened. Nonbeliever...what about this? This ought to make the bones of your body shake, tremble, and scream glory to God and praise to the Father.

We must note there are two princes mentioned in Daniel 9:26. The first is the Messiah Prince "that will be cut off." This prince is

Jesus Christ and being cut off refers to the crucifixion. He had to be killed and raised again the third day (Matthew 16:21). Whosoever believeth in Him should not perish, but have eternal life (John 3:15). The second prince in Daniel 9:26 is "the prince that shall come." This prince is none other than the antichrist. This prince, or antichrist, shall destroy the city of Jerusalem and the sanctuary (verse 26). This prince is also known as the "little horn" in Daniel, Chapter 7. He has also been referred to in other ways in other places in the scriptures as shown below:

1. The King of Fierce (strong) Countenance (Daniel, Chapter 8)
2. The Willful King (Daniel, Chapter 11)
3. The Man of Sin (2 Thessalonians 2:3)
4. The Beast Out of the Sea (Revelation 13:1)
5. To Seal Up the Vision of Prophecy (This has reference to the fulfillment of all prophecy)

Ezekiel had much to say about the millennial temple and the nature of the workshop in the temple. Referring to it as "the most holy place" (Ezekiel 41-46).

In his book, Alva McClain, stated Daniel's prophecy of the seventy weeks has provided an excellent summary of this prophecy.[6] I believe it would be helpful in understanding this prophecy to list the major summary points:

1. The entire prophecy has to do with Daniel's "people" and Daniel's city, that is, the nation of Israel and the city of Jerusalem (Daniel 9:24).
2. Two different princes are mentioned who should not be confused: the first is named Messiah, the Prince (Daniel 9:25); the second is described as the prince that shall come (Daniel 9:26).
3. The entire time period involved is exactly specified as seventy weeks (Daniel 9:24). These seventy weeks are further divided into three lesser periods: (a) a period of seven weeks, afterward

(b) a period of three-score and two weeks, and finally (c) a period of one week (Daniel 9: 25, 27).

4. The beginning of the whole period of the seventy weeks is definitely fixed at "the going forth of the commandment to restore and to build Jerusalem" (Daniel 9:25).

5. The end of the seven weeks and threescore and two weeks (69 weeks) will be marked by the appearance of Messiah as the "Prince" of Israel (Daniel 9:25).

6. At a later time, "after the threescore and two weeks" which follow the first seven weeks (that is after 69 weeks), Messiah the Prince will be cut off," and Jerusalem will again be destroyed by the people of another "prince" who is yet to come (Daniel 9:26).

7. After these two important events, we come to the last or seventieth week. The beginning of which will be clearly marked by the establishment of a firm covenant or treaty between the coming prince and the Jewish nation for a period of "one week" (Daniel 9:27).

8. In the "midst" of this seventieth week, evidently breaking his treaty, the coming prince will suddenly cause the Jewish sacrifice to cease and precipitate upon this people a time of wrath and desolation lasting to the "full end" of the week (Daniel 9:27).

9. With the full completion of the whole period of the seventh weeks, there will be ushered in a time of great and unparalleled blessings for the nation of Israel (Daniel 9:24).

These are nine excellent points of summary of Daniel's prophecy. Chapter nine of the book of Daniel contains some of the most respected and significant prophecy in the entire bible.

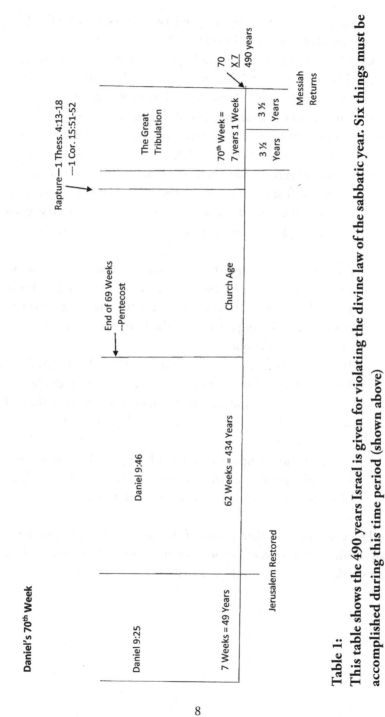

Table 1:
This table shows the 490 years Israel is given for violating the divine law of the sabbatic year. Six things must be accomplished during this time period (shown above)

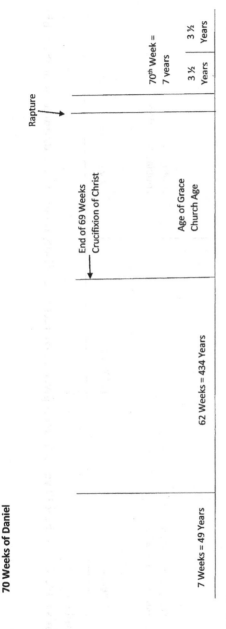

70 Weeks of Daniel

7 Weeks = 49 Years

62 Weeks = 434 Years

End of 69 Weeks
Crucifixion of Christ

Age of Grace
Church Age

Rapture

70th Week =
7 years

3 ½ Years | 3 ½ Years

Table 2:

1. Time given to rebuild the wall and the city of Jerusalem (49 years) (7 weeks)

2. We are now in the Church Age or the Age of Grace. God has stopped the progression of time. The Rapture will start the prophetic clock ticking again. (62 weeks = 434 years)

3. 70th week = 7 years. This is seven years of tribulation.

4. 7 + 62 + 1 = 7 years. (49 + 434 + 7 + 490)

5. Six things must be accomplished by Israel in those "Seventy weeks" or 490 years. These six things have been included in this chapter.

6. The 70th week is often broken into two halves of 3 ½ years each.

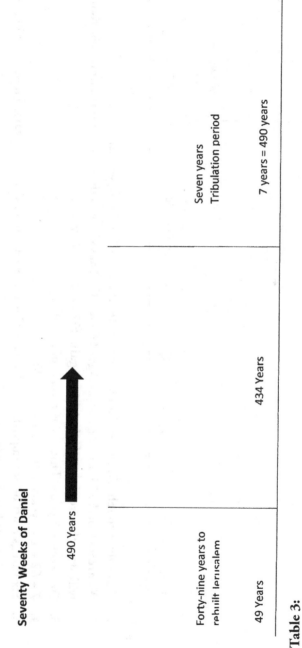

Seventy Weeks of Daniel

490 Years

Forty-nine years to
rebuilt Jerusalem

49 Years

434 Years

Seven years
Tribulation period

7 years = 490 years

Table 3:
This table shows the 490 years Israel is given to correct their disobedience to the divine Law of the Sabbath.

Chapter 2

THE CHURCH AGE

The Church Age is the period of time from Pentecost until the rapture. In the Church Age, God has extended the invitation list beyond the Jews to include the Gentiles and anyone else who will accept His offer of salvation. I am so glad that I was invited to participate in the blessing that God promised Abraham. When Israel rejected Jesus Christ, God turned His attention toward the Gentiles. We must remember this attention is only temporary. In Romans 11, Paul explained that God is not through with Israel. We had better learn to love the land that God promised Abraham because that small country of Israel that we see on the map is not all that God promised Abraham. When Jesus Christ comes back to this earth and sets His feet on the "mount of olives," the greatest earthquake that has ever happened will change the geography of the Middle East. Israel will increase from the River Egypt in the south to Lebanon and Syria in the north. It will increase from the shores of the Mediterranean on the west to the Euphrates River on the east. Psalm 122, verse 6, admonishes us to "pray for the peace of Jerusalem: they shall prosper that love thee." Our prayer should not be so we "shall prosper" but because we love thee. Make this a part of your prayer every day. Israel is going to be alright because the Lord Jesus is in control.

A good way to look at the Church Age is to look at the visibility of the church. The church had its birth at the beginning of Acts, Chapter 2. There are two ways of viewing the church. First, there is the Universal Church. This is the church to which you become a member when you accept Jesus Christ as your Savior. This is the true church of all saved believers. It has members from all over the world. It is the church that will be raptured to heaven by Jesus Christ. This church is made up of Jews and Gentiles who became members by spiritual baptism. Because of this, one could not become a member until Pentecost. The Holy Spirit was not present until then. We are still in the Church Age and will be until the rapture takes place.

A second way to view the church is to look at the local body or the local church. This church consists of all those who attend church on Sunday morning or at other times. Many of these people are or may be saved; many will not. The local church contains both types of individuals. It is helpful to understand the local church by looking at the local churches to which John was writing. These seven churches possessed all the characteristics of all the other seven. They were also unique in that they possessed characteristics that none of the others possessed. They were really "ideal types" which would allow the comparison of each one to all the others. For example, we are living in the Laodicean time. There are characteristics of this church that are unique only to this church. There are dominating characteristics of this church. All the other churches had some of these characteristics but they were not dominating in the other churches. The most dominating characteristic of the church at Laodicea is apostasy. Apostasy is the falling away from the true doctrine of the church. The falling away from the faith. The Laodicean church is a description of the apostasy that will take place in the last days. All the other churches possessed some apostasy but it was not a dominating characteristic. Characteristics of the Laodicean church increased "from about 1900 to the present day. This is the age of the church of the apostasy." [1] We are definitely living in the last days of the Laodicean church. Wherever you and I attend church, we are seeing some of this falling away. Many churches have made the church a social institution. The church serves a different purpose and this is apostasy. The church has already taken second place. If we are living in the last days, and I believe we are, this trend toward apostasy will continue to increase. After the true church has been raptured to heaven, the church that has been left behind will be the total apostate church.

From the time John wrote the first letter to the church at Ephesus until he wrote the letter to the Church at Laodicea, all churches had some of the characteristics of all the others. This will be true during any period of history. Although one characteristic will dominate during any particular period of history. So, all seven types can be found all the way up to the rapture. Jesus found things wrong in all except in two letters. The church at Philadelphia was one of these churches in which Jesus could find no wrong. This church was in existence during the great missionary movement from A.D. 1648-1900. The church at Smyrna was the only other church that satisfied Jesus and one in which he could find no wrong.

I can surely see apostasy in churches all around us. The apostasy will continue to increase. It indicates we are truly living in the last days before the rapture takes place. I believe the rapture is near.

I have come to believe that we have not given the deserved strong attention to the seven letters to the seven churches in understanding the Church Age from Pentecost to the rapture. There is a verse in the book of Revelation that would support this claim. The verse is repeated several times (Revelation, Chapter 2:7, 11, 17, 29; Chapter 3:6,13,22). "He who has an ear, let him hear what the spirit says to the churches." [2] If we study these seven churches, we will find a pattern of the churches all across the church age and all the way to the church at Laodicea. As we know, the Laodicean church was characterized by apostasy. This is one reason we can know that we are living in the end times. There is apostasy in most churches around us. Look at the church you attend. Why is it so hard to get people to attend Sunday school where the Bible is being taught? Why is it so hard to get people to attend Wednesday night classes where prophecy is being taught? The answer to these two questions is obvious.

In G. H. Pember's book, *Great Prophecies of the Bible*, Mr. Pember lists the seven churches and the characteristics of each one. [7] They are as follows:

Ephesus = Relaxation. The waning of love at the close of apostolic times.

Smyrna = Bitterness; also myrrh, an unguent especially used for embalming the dead. The epoch of the ten great persecutions.

Pergamum = A tower. Earthly greatness of the nominal church from the accession of Constantinea.

Thyatira = She that is unwearied in sacrifices. The catholic churches, with their perpetually repeated sacrifice of the mass.

Sardis = Renovation. The result of the reformation.

Philadelphia = Brotherly love. The gathering in of those who believe the love of Christ to be a stronger bond of union than any ties of sect. This gathering evidently involves preparation for the Lord's return.

Laodicea = The custom, or judgment, of the people. The period in which the people constitute themselves judges of what is right and so altogether set aside the word of God. They are, consequently, rejected of the Lord Jesus.

The following is a list of the seven churches and their date in history: [8]

Ephesus	(A.D.30-100)	Apostolic Church
Smyrna	(100-313)	Roman Persecution
Pergamum	(313-600)	Age of Constantine
Thyatira	(600-1517)	Dark Ages
Sardis	(1517-1648)	Reformation
Philadelphia	(1648-1900)	Missionary Movement
Laodicea	(1900-present)	Apostasy

The New Testament church clearly speaks about the last days of the church in the epistles (New Testament letters to the church). Virtually all of these comments about the last days apostasy were written shortly before the death of each apostle writing (that is, during the last days of the various apostles), as if to emphasize the dangers blatant during the church's last days. [9] Every one of these passages emphasizes over and over again that the greatest characteristic of the final time of the church will be that of apostasy.[10]

1. I Timothy 4:1-3

Apostasy is taking place within the organized local churches among those who have earlier professed faith in the Lord Jesus Christ and the true doctrine. In the very first verse of Chapter 4, Timothy is saying that some are being pulled away from true doctrine by seducing spirits and doctrines of devils. He is speaking of the churches of today because he uses the phrase "in the latter times." Timothy is teaching that in the latter times, there will be teachers who will mislead a large number of people who will depart from the faith. Apostasy will continue to increase in churches until the rapture takes place leaving behind a large apostate church. Do you know that you know that you know and are you strong enough to recognize these demonic spirits? Many today are being pulled away from the true doctrine by false teaching and the doctrine of demonic spirits. Remember our salvation is through the death, burial, and resurrection of Jesus Christ.

2. 2 Timothy 3:1-5

In these versus, Timothy is using the phrase "the last days." Days just before the rapture. False teachers will enter the church speaking perverse things. Perilous times shall come. These verses present the best scriptural picture of what the church looks like today. J. Vernon McGee gives nineteen words or phrases that describes the last days from these versus. [11]

A. Lovers of their own selves… "self lovers"
B. Covetous….lovers of money. I Timothy 6:10….the love of money is the root of all evil. It is our attitude toward money.
C. Boasters
D. Proud…haughty
E. Blasphemers
F. Disobedient to parents
G. Unthankful – many people never even thank God
H. Unholy
I. Without natural affection…having abnormal relationships. Today, homosexuality is being accepted as normal.
J. Truth breakers…people who are impossible to get along with. Do you know any?
K. False accusers
L. Incontinent …without self control
M. Fierce…savage
N. Despisers of those who are good
O. Traitors….betrayers
P. Heady…reckless
Q. High-minded…drunk with pride
R. Lovers of pleasures more than lovers of our day
S. Having a form of godliness but denying the power thereof… from such turn away

3. 2 Timothy 4:3-4

The time will come when people will not endure sound doctrine including church members. Today, it seems church members shape their preacher. Members go to church to close their eyes and eye the clothes.

4. James 5:1-8

These verses direct our attention toward the way we make and manage our own money. If we make our riches in a dishonest way by stepping on others, robbing the poor, or mistreating other Christians, God will judge these actions. This should serve as a warning to great corporations, labor unions, and even great church organizations that God will judge the way they spend their money.

5. 2 Peter 2

Peter uses this entire chapter to help us understand how a church may become characterized by apostasy. There were false prophets and false teachers among the people in Israel. There are false prophets and false teachers among believers in the church today. Not only do teachers need to be checked today but also those who are authors of the books you are reading as well as those individuals you watch on television. People today are easily deceived. False teachers today are teaching things they know are not true. What are the reasons teachers, writers, and preachers are teaching things they deliberately know is false? For many, it is for big egos and arrogance. Many believe they have to be this way so the people will accept them. Maybe it is for selfish reasons. They do it for money. Many of the teachers and preachers know they are presenting a false front but they want to be popular. They know how to use flowery language in teaching what is contrary to true doctrine. These teachers, preachers, and writers are turning the true doctrine into a false doctrine. Our churches today are becoming apostate churches. This is a major sign of the end times.

6. 2 Peter 3:3-7

In these verses, Peter is helping us to understand specifically who the apostates are. In verse 3, he calls them "scoffers." Scoffers will be members of the churches. They will also be teachers and pastors whose hearts are not in true doctrine. These churches will be the apostate churches after the true church has been raptured to heaven.

7. Jude

Apostasy is a departure from faith in true doctrine. Although the departure had already begun when Jude was writing this book; Apostasy was not of the magnitude that it is today. Apostasy has slipped into our churches and is doing more damage than anyone can recognize. Both Paul and Jude gave us great warnings about apostasy in the last days. Today, apostasy is evident and present. It is not difficult to determine if our preachers and teachers are godly men. Look at the immorality of our day. The danger is that our churches condone immorality. There are churches today that approve of immorality. Will we be judged because we accept immorality? God judged Sodom and Gomorrah for their acceptance. Are we turning from the true doctrine of God's word? This is apostasy. In today's society, it seems many people are leaving God's standards out of marriage (allowing same sex marriages), birth (by condoning abortion), prayer (not understanding the importance of prayer), the bible (banning bible reading in public places), total government overreach into our lives (where is our freedom of religion, freedom of worship, freedom of education in the workplace?). The list is endless. I like what John Hagee says "we had better pack up, pray up, and look up, because we are about to go up." As I have said before, the greatest characteristic of the final time of the church will be that of apostasy.

J. Dwight Pentecost presents a more specific way of looking at the conditions within the church in the last days. [12] These conditions within the church are presented as a system of denials. They are as follows:

1.	Denial of God	Luke 17:26, 2 Timothy 3:4,5
2.	Denial of Christ	1 John 2:18; 4:3, 2 Peter 2:6
3.	Denial of Christ's return	2 Peter 3:3,4
4.	Denial of the faith	1 Timothy 4: 1,2; Jude 3
5.	Denial of sound doctrine	2 Timothy 4:3-4
6.	Denial of the separated life	1 Timothy 3:1-7
7.	Denial of Christian liberty	1 Timothy 4:3-4
8.	Denial of morals	2 Timothy 3:1-8, 13; Jude 18
9.	Denial of authority	2 Timothy 3:4

These denials certainly depict the day in which we live. The lack of morals and respect for authority continue to increase. Earlier in my life, we did not hear much filthy language nor was there much challenge of authority. Go back to the decade of the 50's and homosexual behavior was not at all visible. Same sex marriages were non-existent. To challenge authority brought serious consequences. These and the other conditions are fully present in today's churches. All of these conditions will be present just before the tribulation time indicating that we are living in the end times. Look at how close we may be to the rapture of the church. Apostasy is a major sign of the end of the age just before Jesus Christ comes back for the rapture of the church. All of the doctrines listed above are highly visible in our churches today. Many church going people are unhappy with their church.

In my judgment, we are at the end of the church age. The church you attend will certainly not get you to heaven. What will get you to heaven is your personal relationship with Jesus Christ and what he did at Calvary. Ask him to forgive you of your sins and turn your life over to him and believe that he rose from the dead and lives today...then you will be ready for the rapture. Are you rapture ready? I hope you are. Hallelujah!

For so many people the debate goes on about when God intervened in this earth and the creation of this earth had its beginning. There have been theories put forward to explain various thoughts about when God began with the creation of the earth. Remember, this earth was at one time void and without form. God changed that. How long ago? Who has the answer? This writing is not intended to get involved in answering all those questions. For me, I accept completely and satisfyingly the Christian world's explanation of the age of the earth. That is, God's intervention into the creation of the earth as we know it is about 6,000 years old. The earth could be millions of years old but that is not what I believe. There is an explanation upon which this thought is based and a scripture that supports the explanation. That scripture is 2 Peter 3:8 which says *"But beloved, be not ignorant of this one thing, that one day is with the Lord as a thousand years, and a thousand years as one day."* [13]

The scriptural illustration and support for this explanation is as follows:

1 2	2 Days	Creation to Flood	2,000
3 4	4 Days	Flood to Birth of Jesus	2,000
5 6	6 Days	Birth of Jesus to Second Coming	2,000
7	1 Day	Millennium	1,000
			7,000

I believe this explanation helps us to understand just where we are at this point in time. God took six days to create the heavens and the earth. He rested on the seventh day. One day equals 1,000 years. It took 6,000 years to get to God's second coming. God will rest for 1,000 years. The number "7" means completion or perfection. The end of this millennium will be completion. It has been 2,000 years since the birth of Christ. We are definitely living in the end times. For clarification:

1. The number "7" means completion or perfection.
2. 7,000 years represents the ending of the millennium and will be completion or perfection.
3. It has been 2,000 years since the birth of Christ and that means we are definitely living in the end times.
4. One day equals 1,000 years.

5. God took six days to create the heavens and earth.
6. God rested on the seventh day.
7. It took 6,000 years to get to God's second coming (rapture).
8. God will rest for 1,000 (millennium).
9. According to this explanation, we are definitely living in the end times.

Chapter 3

THE RETURN OF JESUS CHRIST

The second coming of Jesus Christ to this earth is one of the most significant events mentioned in the entire bible. The New Testament alone includes 321 references to this awesome occurrence making it the second most prominent doctrine presented in scripture. The first being salvation. I have been attending church all my life and the second coming of Jesus Christ to this earth to set up his kingdom and the rapture are the least taught topics in the bible. People have but a vague understanding of these two doctrines. It is because these topics are just not preached from the pulpit nor taught in classes. This is interesting because almost one third of the bible is prophecy. I believe if you ask members of many church congregations today if they had ever heard the word "rapture," their reply would be no.

Reference to the second coming is found throughout the bible. Enoch, in Jude 14 and 15, was the first prophet to mention the second coming.[14] Reference to the second coming has been found in the book of Psalms, and mentioned by prophets and the apostles. Jesus also talked about the second coming on several occasions. If Jesus did not return to earth he would be guilty of lying since he promised many times in scripture that he would return. If he does not return, he would be guilty of deception. Remember, God cannot lie. He promised in John 14:3 that he would return. This verse says *"and if I go and prepare a place for you, I will come again and receive you unto myself; that where I am there ye may be also."*

The Rapture (That Blessed Hope)

We must remember the return of Jesus Christ will occur in two phases. The first phase is the rapture (that blessed hope). The second phase is the coming of Jesus Christ to earth (the glorious appearing). Titus 2:13

The next item on God's prophetic calendar is the rapture. No date is given in the scripture for when the rapture will take place; however, the second coming of Jesus Christ to the earth will be about seven years after the rapture. I use the word "about" because there is no doubt that there will be a period of time between the rapture and the start of the seven years tribulation. This will be a short period of time of only a few weeks or months. The antichrist will come on the scene and sign a peace covenant with Israel. The signing of this peace covenant will start the seven years tribulation period. The second coming of Jesus Christ to this earth will be seven years from the time of this signing. We can determine when the second coming (the glorious appearing) will occur but we do not know when the rapture will take place.

The word "rapture" itself does not appear in the bible. The rapture is certainly a central theme of prophecy. The rapture is simply the sudden and instant removal of all saved people, dead or alive, who will have their immortal bodies transferred from this earth to meet Jesus in the air (1 Thessalonians 4:17). The English word rapture comes from the Latin word raptus. In the Latin bible, the word raptus translates the Greek word harpazo which means to siege upon with force or to snatch up or be caught up or caught away. In any case, the church will in a moment of time, in the twinkling of an eye (1 Corinthians 15:52), rise up to meet Jesus in the air. It has been determined the twinkling of an eye has been measured to be 11/100 of a second. If you thought it would take a long time to get those individuals who were saved but are now deceased as well as those who are saved and still alive to heaven to meet Jesus, you can now rest at ease. It will take Jesus less than a second to get the church, his bride, up in the clouds to meet him in the air. What a trip for the saints. We will get our new bodies as we rise to meet Jesus in the air. I have mentioned to classes that I have taught that I will have to have a new body because this current old body could not take it when I see Jesus face-to-face. I would certainly have a heart attack. I know it is going to be awesome with a new body. I cannot wait. I love him and I am longing to see him. Remember, we are going up with our saved family members and with so many dear, dear, friends who are saved. Many of these are already with Jesus through death. They will still go up to meet Jesus in the air. They will also get their new bodies as they rise. To be absent from the body is to be present with him (Jesus) (Corinthians 5:8).

On the Resurrected Body

There are so many topics of interest to the Christian that we never hear fully discussed, preached, or taught. Recently, I was part of a discussion on the resurrection particularly on what the resurrected body would be like. Obviously, there were varied and different views on this topic. When we get into discussions on these kinds of topics, our views and thinking should be based on scripture and not on what we hope. What does the scripture say? A good place to start in understanding what our new and glorified body will be like is found in Luke 24: 39-41. In this chapter, Jesus appeared to the disciples in Jerusalem. In verse 39, Jesus says *"behold my hands and my feet, that it is I myself: handle me, and see; for a spirit hath not flesh and bone, as ye see me have."* Jesus is establishing that he is a body of substance. "Behold my hands and my feet; handle me; see me that it is I myself." He was saying, I'm not a spirit or a ghost. He also asked for something to eat and they gave him a piece of broiled fish and a piece of honeycomb and he ate. I don't know if our new bodies will have to eat but it will have the capacity to eat. In these versus, we see that Jesus had hands and feet. He had the sense of feel and touch and he could see. We, too, in our new bodies will be able to do all these things. If he ate, he could surely taste what he was eating. We know there will be singing in heaven so we will have ears to hear. Psalm 150 is a psalm of praise. There are also references to singing in Isaiah, Revelation, and other places. I believe our new bodies will possess the senses and they will be more intense and sensitive than in our earthly bodies.

One question that everybody wants answered is: Will we know each other in heaven? The answer is yes. We won't know less in heaven than we know on earth. We will know more. Our new body will even have a resemblance to our earthly body. If when I get to heaven, I am something else or someone else, who am I? Jesus said in Luke 24:39 "It is I myself!" Jesus replied to Mary by calling her name in John 20:16. Then she turned and said to him in Hebrew "Rabbone!" (which means teacher or master). Mary recognized the voice of Jesus. This means that in our new bodies, our voices will sound like our voices on earth. Mary embraced him (John 20:17). She embraced a physical body, a body of substance. Jesus told the disciples in John 24:39 that his body was "flesh and bones." The other women who came to the tomb a second time were met there by Jesus and they held his feet (Matthew 28:9). The women could see the nail prints in his feet and they recognized him as the one who died on the cross. In John 20:28, Thomas recognized Jesus was who he said he was and Thomas answered "my Lord and my God!" Those words are so powerful. Jesus called Thomas by his name. In heaven, we will be called by the names we go by on earth. In heaven, Abraham, Isaac, Jacob, Moses, Joseph, David, Paul, my parents, my family (praise God), my many loved ones will go by their names because their name is their identity. We will not lose our identity because that is who we are. Randy Alcorn notes in his book *Heaven* that we will receive new names in heaven (Isaiah 62:2; 65:15; Revelation 2:17, 3:12). New names do not invalidate the old ones. Many people had multiple names in scripture: Jacob is also Israel; Simon is also Peter; Saul is also Paul. [15]

I believe our new bodies will be real substantive physical bodies. Our resurrected Christ is our model and he had a real physical body. Our new bodies will be perfect. Many bible scholars and students believe "as each person reaches their peak of perfection around the age of 30, they will be resurrected as they would have appeared at that time even if they never lived to reach that age." [16] John Walvoord would agree. He says that it is probably that in resurrection our bodies will be improved, and older people will be returned to comparative youth at about 30 years of age.[17] Hank Hanegroaff says that "our DNA is programmed in such a way that at a particular point, we reach optimal development from a functional perspective somewhere at around 30. If the blueprint of our glorified bodies is in the DNA, then it would stand to reason that our bodies will be resurrected at the optimal stage of development determined by our DNA." [18] In 1 John 3:2 it says "Beloved, now we are children of God, and it has not appeared as yet what we shall be. We know that, when he appears, we shall be like him, because we shall see him just as he is." [19] It is impossible to know all that our new body will be but the bible gives us enough information on some things about our new body. For example, the bible says our new bodies will be flesh and bones. We will have a physical body that can see, hear, eat, travel long distances at the speed of thought, and have the ability to go through walls. Our new bodies will not experience pain or sickness and there will be no tears. Our new bodies cannot sin and we will never be tempted to sin. We will maintain our gender in heaven because our gender is part of who we are. Jesus was not genderless after his resurrection. No one thought him to be a woman or as androgynous. What we know about our new bodies is so great but will be so much more than we can even imagine.

The transfiguration of Christ is another example that leads us to believe we will recognize people in heaven. The Disciples of Christ recognized Moses and Elijah and they had never seen these two men before. The scripture of 1 Thessalonians 4:14-18 would lose some of its hope and emotion if we did not recognize our loved ones. We have been singing about that "reunion" in the air for years. I am convinced people who are alive when Jesus returns will at once know those who have already been taken to heaven and those already in heaven will at once know their loved ones who were raised. They will go up together to meet Jesus in the air.

I agree with John Hagee when he says "I do not know exactly how my supernatural body will be formed, but I know that it will be recognizable." [20] The bible says that in eternity, *"I shall know just as I am known."* (I Corinthians 13:12) Our new bodies will look very much as we look now. We will be able to recognize one another. Our new bodies will be perfectly healthy. We will not have to take all the medications we take today. Our new bodies will not be subject to disease such as heart disease, diabetes, asthma, osteoporosis, arthritis, cancer, MS, HIV. There are about 15 million diabetics in America and many have to take insulin injections daily. There could be that many more and they just do not know it yet. Unfortunately, we all know people who have fought disease of one type or another. It will be wonderful when disease is no longer a threat to our lives. King David prayed in Psalm 139:14 *"I praise you because I am fearfully and wonderfully made."* [21] In John 20:19, it is indicated that our new bodies will be able to go through walls. Jesus did. Our new bodies will be able to travel at the speed of thought. Jesus did. Remember the story of the two disciples at Emmaus? (Luke 24:31). Jesus was able to defy gravity (Acts 1:9).

The resurrected body will have resemblance to that which is buried but it will be raised with more perfection and with different qualities. John Walvoord states: [22]

Earthly Body	*Resurrection Body*
Sown a perishable body	Raised an imperishable body
Sown in dishonor	Raised in glory
Sown in weakness	Raised in power
Sown a natural body	Raised a spiritual body

I am so looking forward to standing before Jesus in my new body that will be so magnificent that I cannot comprehend how great it will actually be. Neither can I comprehend, even though I have tried, what it will be like to live with Jesus, King David, Moses, Abraham, Joseph, Job, Isaac, Jacob, Paul, Peter, my family, and other loved ones for eternity. I am ready, are you?

We will receive our new bodies the instant Jesus Christ call us home in the rapture. Our bodies will be changed in the "twinkling of an eye." [23] I believe an angel will be right there to give us a white robe to wear to meet Jesus in the air because we cannot wear our earthly clothes in heaven. Nothing made on earth will enter heaven (only the nail prints in his hands). Our robe will be white because heaven's clothes are white. It may be decorated with gold, silver, purple, blue, and maybe pearls and precious stones. It will be a beautiful robe.

When I study, teach, sing or write, I often think of a song a friend of mine wrote some time ago entitled "Family Reunion." I also think of a song I have been singing all of my life entitled "Reunion In Heaven." I know there will be a reunion in heaven. I do not know if that reunion will take place as we go up to see Jesus at the rapture or if it will be after Jesus takes us on to heaven. My friend had these thoughts (author, Steve Slaton-see permission in records):

I'm gonna look for mama, I'm gonna look for dad.
I'm gonna find all the friends that I've ever had.
Lord, I hope nobody's missing.
I pray their all prepared.

I'm gonna look for my daughter.
I'm gonna look for my son.
But first, I'm gonna find my Jesus,
And praise Him for what He's done.

Chorus
We're gonna have a family reunion,
At my Father's house.
With my brothers and sisters, up beyond the clouds.
What a happy day in heaven, I know it's gonna be.
When we gather with His children,
At that family reunion.

I'm gonna look for Moses, I'm gonna look for Job.
I'm gonna find the apostles, as I stroll those streets of gold.
There's gonna be a celebration,
This world has never known.
I'm gonna stand before the throne, in my unworthiness.
And claim the blood of Jesus for He is my righteousness.

I know that when we get up in the clouds to meet Jesus in the air, he will take us on to New Jerusalem (heaven). New Jerusalem will be far beyond the moon and stars but it won't take us long to get there because our new bodies will be able to travel at the speed of thought.

Frequently, a friend of mine and I get to talking about how wonderful it will be to see Jesus and our family. He then said he wants to see the apostle Paul. He will rank order those he wants to see. I agree with him and then I have certain friends that I want to see. I sang in a quartet with several of them for several years. I get so hungry to see them sometimes. I am so longing and looking forward for the rapture to take place. Can you imagine all the associations you've had in your lifetime and being able to sing and worship with all of them in heaven?

Dress

The question has been asked "What will we be wearing when we go up to meet Jesus in the air"? That is a good question. When men die, they are buried in a beautiful suit. When women die, they are buried in a beautiful dress. Then there are those who are lost in fires or in large bodies of water or cremated. If they were saved when they died, they will be brought back to life and their soul and spirit that have been in paradise will be joined with their bodies and those bodies will be instantly transformed or changed into new bodies. All who are dead in Christ will be given, in a moment, a "NEW" body. Those who are saved and alive when Jesus returns will be changed and given a "NEW" body in the twinkling of an eye. None of us who are going up to meet Jesus in the air at the rapture will go up wearing our earthly clothes. Nothing that is made by hands will get into heaven. Nor will we go up to meet Jesus naked. So at the moment we are given our new bodies, I believe that an angel will be right there to give us a white robe. I believe these robes will be beautifully decorated. After all, angels serve him and he has riches beyond compare. This is a major, major event. God has told his son to go get my children. We are also the bride of Christ. Does scripture support what I have just said? I believe it does.

If we look at Revelation 7:9, it says *"After this I beheld, and lo, a great multitude, which no man could number, of all nations, and kindreds, and people, and tongues, stood before the throne, and before the lamb, clothed with white robes, and palms in their hands* [24] Sounds like to me the church has been raptured to heaven. Look at this verse. So many millions standing before the throne of God and before the lamb that no man could number. They were clothed with white robes. This is surely the church, the bride of Christ, which has been raptured to heaven. I thank you, Lord Jesus, that I am one in this number. So are my mom, dad, brother, two sisters, and some precious, precious friends. Revelation 7:10-13 says *"and cried with a loud voice, saying, salvation to our God which sitteth upon the throne, and unto the lamb."* [25] *And all the angels stood round about the throne, and about the elders and the four beasts, and fell before the throne on their faces, and worshipped God saying, amen: "blessing, and glory, and wisdom, and thanksgiving, and honor, and power, and might, be unto our God forever and ever. Amen."* [26] *And one of the elders answered, saying unto me, what are these which are arrayed in white robes? And whence came they?* In this verse, look at all those who are around the throne (1) All the angels stood around the throne. There are probably millions of angels in heaven. Note, the angels stood. I do not believe a spirit can stand nor is a spirit visible. Here they stood around the throne. (2) The 24 elders were there. (3) The four living creatures were there. I'm not sure the living creatures have ever been defined. They all fell on their faces and worshiped God. They were truly worshipping God. They were saying blessing and glory and wisdom and thanksgiving and honor and power and might be to our God forever and ever.

In my research, I was unable to find saints wearing any other color but white. Following is a compilation of the use of white. This may not be exhaustive but does provide very strong evidence for our dress in heaven.

(1) Revelation 7:9

After these things I looked, and lo, a great multitude, which no man could number, out of all nations and kindreds and people and tongues, stood before the throne and before the lamb, clothes with white robes, with palms in their hands. [27]

The reason I believe this verse is about the rapture is because there are going to be saved people from all over the world in the rapture. From every nation. A second reason is because in this verse there will be a great multitude, millions and millions, no doubt, which no man could count. A third reason is because I'm not sure there is any other place in the bible where a multitude that no man could number is together in that place standing before the throne of God and before the lamb. And they are all clothed with "white" robes. They also have palms in their hand. This stands for victory and certainly these saints have been victorious.

(2) Revelation 7:10-12

All angels, the 24 elders, the four living creatures, and they fell before the throne on their faces and worshipped God...... [28]

These verses tells us of others who are standing around the throne of God.

(3) Revelation 7:13-14

And one of the elders answered, saying to me (John), who are these people who are arrayed in "white" robes, and where do they come from? And I said to him, sir, you know. And he said to me, these are the ones who came out of the great tribulation and have washed their robes, and have "whitened" them in the blood of the lamb. [29]

In these verses, we see "white robes" referenced two times by one of the elders. These verses indicated here the saints are now in heaven and all are wearing "white robes." They received their robes, given to them by angels, the moment they were transformed to meet Jesus in the air.

(4) Revelation 19:8

And to her was granted that she should be arrayed in fine linen, clean and "white": for the fine linen is the righteousness of saints. [30]

In this verse, the "she" is the lamb. The lamb is the church or the "bride of Christ." The bride is already in heaven and the marriage is about to take place. This verse says that the bride "should be arrayed in fine linen, clean and "white".... [31] So the bride of Christ is going to be wearing "white" at this marriage.

(5) Revelation 6:9-11

And when he had opened the fifth seal, I saw under the alter the souls of them that were slain for the word of God, and for the testimony which they held: And they cried with a loud voice saying, how long, O Lord, holy and true, dost thou not judge and avenge our blood on them that dwell on the earth? And "white robes" were given unto every one of them; and it was said unto them that they should rest yet for a little season until their fellow servants also and their brethren that should be killed as they were should be fulfilled. [32]

In these verses, we find another group that has been given "white robes." This gives support that our dress in heaven will be "white robes." This text speaks of a group of saints that have not yet been raptured nor will they ever be. They have given their lives for the word of God. They are saved tribulation martyrs and they have been given "white robes" and told to wait for a little season. I believe these tribulation martyrs are already in paradise because II Corinthians 5:8 tells us *to be absent from the body is to be present with the Lord* [33] Revelation 20:4 says *and I saw the souls of them that were beheaded for the witness of Jesus, and for the word of God, and which had not worshipped the beast, neither his image, neither had received his mark upon their foreheads, or in their hands; and they lived and reigned with Christ a thousand years.* These tribulation martyrs will be resurrected during that 75 day period from the time Jesus Christ comes back to earth to stop Armageddon until he sets up his millennial kingdom. [34]

(6) Revelation 19:14

And the armies which were in heaven followed him upon white horses, clothed in fine linen, white and clean. [35]

This verse provides additional support for the clothes that we will wear in heaven will be "white." This verse is describing the return of Jesus Christ to earth at the second coming or the glorious appearing. The armies of heaven (or the saints) following Jesus and the horses they are riding are even white. White robes are never given to sinful bodies. At the beginning of the rapture white robes are given only after bodies are changed from mortal to immortal bodies. When we get our NEW bodies they will be new bodies that cannot sin. The new body will not have a sin nature. Immortality means our new bodies will never die. Our new bodies will never experience pain. We will have 20/20 vision so no one will have to wear glasses (see topic on new body). As already stated, this study was not exhaustive but this search never found any other color but white for our clothing in heaven.

(7) Revelation 3:5

He that overcometh, the same shall be clothes in white raiment; and I will not blot out his name out of the book of life, but I will confess his name before my father, and before his angels. [36]

These verses provide strong evidence of the color of our dress. As soon as we are given our new bodies when we are raptured, we will also be given a white robe to wear. I believe that immediately after we are given our new bodies, an angel will be right there to fit us with a new white robe to wear as we go up to meet Jesus in the air. How great is that as we look toward our immediate future?

(8) Revelation 3:18

I council thee to buy of me gold tried in the fire, that thou mayest be rich; and white raiment that thou mayest be clothed, and that the shame of the nakedness do not appear; and anoint thine eyes with eye salve, that thou mayest see. [37]

These verses indicate the clothing of both the elders and all the church age saints are clothed in white.

(9) Acts 1:9-11

And when he had spoken these things, while they beheld, he was taken up; and a cloud received him out of their sight. And while they looked steadfastly toward heaven as he went up, behold two men stood by them in white apparel which also said, ye men of Galilee, why stand ye gazing up into heaven? This same Jesus which is taken up from you into heaven, shall so come in like manner as ye have seen him go into heaven. [38]

These two men dressed in white apparel were probably Enoch and Elijah. Their dress reveals heaven's dress.

Imminency

Imminency is a concept that teaches that Jesus Christ could return for his church at any moment. The rapture of the church is the first phase of the return of Jesus Christ to this earth. There are no signs or warnings necessary for the return of Jesus Christ. His return is imminent. It could happen at any moment. That is the way we define imminency. Webster's dictionary defines imminent as "an event that is likely to take place soon or about to happen." [39] As it is issued with regard to the rapture it does not have to be soon. The scripture just does not give us a date for when the rapture will take place. Many bible scholars believe the return of Christ for his church may be soon...even sooner than we think. I believe the return of our Lord will be very soon.

Dr. Renald Showers defines an imminent event as one which is always hanging overhead. It is constantly ready to befall or overtake one; close at hand in its incident. [40] Nothing else must take place before the imminent event takes place. If something must take place before the imminent event happens, that would destroy the concept of imminency.

How awesome is God's plan? He realized the problems that would be created by giving a date for his return. Look at the following problems:

1. If God set a date for his return, everybody would just wait until about a week before his return to get saved. Just look at what this would do to God's plan.
    A. People would not study the bible so they would not learn from his word. We would never know what he expects of Christians. We would never know the blessings of our salvation.
    B. We would never know what Jesus did for our salvation at Calvary.
    C. We would never know the nature of his suffering on the cross.
    D. We would never know the awesomeness of his love for us.
    E. We would never have anyone to call upon to help us during times of sadness. My wife and I have lost our parents. I do not know how you make it through times of death without having the Lord Jesus to call upon. Having saintly Christian parents makes this time easier.
    F. We would not know the blessing of walking through each day with the Lord Jesus.

2. To set a date for the rapture would result in chaos in the world.
   A. We would not have God's love in our hearts and we would not know how to love each other. We would not have Christian brothers and sisters to love.
   B. The divorce rate would be much higher. Love for family members would be weaker.
   C. Crime rates would soar due to murder, alcoholism, drugs, and child abuse because in the absence of love is hate. In heaven everybody will love everybody.
   D. Deceit of all kinds would be rampant (including the church).
   E. There would be no trust, honor, and dignity.
   F. Even the necessary work of a society would not get done.
   G. Fear would be pervasive in all segments of society. Fear would permeate every institution in society.

God knew what he was doing when he made this part of his plan. He knew what would be best for all mankind. The doctrine of imminency supports the doctrine of pretribulationism. What gives support for a pretribulation rapture is that the rapture could take place at any moment. That is the doctrine of imminency. At any moment the rapture is imminent. I believe that a pretribulation rapture has the strongest scripture support of all other views. There are other views as to when the rapture will take place. The post tribulation view is no doubt the most popular view. However, it lacks strong scriptural support.

Views of the Rapture

There are several views as to when the rapture will take place. I believe it is necessary to define these various views so that we will have a better understanding of imminency, the rapture, and what the scripture teaches us about something as important as the rapture. It boggles my mind to learn that there are people all around us that know nothing about the rapture nor what will happen to them when we reach the end of the church age. There is so much lack of knowledge and misunderstanding about the doctrines of imminency, rapture, and the church age. I hope with this study, we can have a much better and clearer understanding of these doctrines.

1.   Pre-Tribulation View

I believe that this view is more strongly supported by scripture. It is doctrine that states the rapture will take place before the start of the end-time tribulation. There are scriptures which teach the church will be raptured before the seven years tribulation period starts. God makes several definite promises that the church will not have to go through the wrath of the tribulation. For example:

A.   Revelation 3:10

> *Because thou has kept the word of my patience, I also will keep thee from the hour of temptation, which shall come upon all the world, to try them that dwell upon the earth.* [41]

This is a promise of a removing from a time of testing. This verse uses the phrase "the hour of temptation" which is referring to the seven years tribulation period. The church is delivered from the wrath to come.

B.   1 Thessalonians 1:10

> *And to wait for his son from heaven, whom he raised from the dead, even Jesus, which delivered us from the "wrath to come."* [42]

We are not looking for the tribulation "the last week of Daniel" to start. Rather, we are looking for "that blessed hope (Titus 2:13). We will not be here when the wrath of the tribulation begins. We will already be in heaven.

C. 1 Thessalonians 5:9

For God hath not appointed us to wrath, but to obtain salvation by our Lord Jesus Christ. [43]

There are 21 reasons that point to a pretribulation rapture view. I believe these 21 reasons to be so powerful that any bible student would do well to do an in-depth research on each view.

D. Romans 5:19-35

E. Luke 21:36

2. Mid-Tribulation Rapture

This view holds that the church will be raptured at the midpoint of Daniel's seventh week. Revelation 3:10 is fulfilled by this view because the wrath of God does not start until the midpoint of the seven years tribulation. The wrath of God is poured out upon the entire world for 3 ½ years (the last 3 ½ years of the seven year tribulation). The church is raptured at that point thus it is kept from the hour of temptation. This view also holds that the church will go through the first 3 ½ years of the seven year tribulation.

Mid-tribulationists believe there are definite signs associated with the rapture. This does not have to be true with pre-tribulationism. The pre-tribulation rapture is a sign less rapture. These signs include:

A. False christs
B. Wars and rumors of wars
C. Famines
D. Earthquakes
E. Hatred, persecution, martyrdom
F. Apostasy
G. Survival of the remnant
H. Worldwide spread of the gospel

I. Building of a temple in Jerusalem

J. Enthronement of the antichrist in the temple in Jerusalem

The mid-tribulationists do not believe the rapture can take place until these events happen. [44]

There are major and significant flaws with the mid-tribulation view. Mark Hitchcock lists four in his book *The End*. [45]

(1) The trumpets in 1 Corinthians 15:52 and Revelation 11:15 should not be considered as the same. They are not. Because the trumpet in 1 Corinthians 15 is called the "last" trumpet, it does not mean it is the last trumpet in God's whole prophetic program. The last trumpet of the rapture is the final trumpet of this church age and it will summon God's people to the great reunion in the sky. The last trumpet argument undermines the mid-tribulation view.

(2) The mid-tribulation view denies the doctrine of imminency. The doctrine of imminency says Christ could return at any moment and there are no prophetic events that must transpire ahead of the rapture. If the mid-trib view is correct and Christ cannot return until the midpoint of the tribulation, then there are prophecies that must be fulfilled before Christ can return. This view destroys the doctrine of imminency.

(3) The mid-tribulation view holds that Christians will not go through the wrath of God that is poured out on the earth. Wrath begins at the midpoint of the seven years tribulation. Revelation 6:16-17 references God's wrath and this occurs long before the seventh trumpet of Revelation 11:15.

(4) There is a disagreement among the mid-tribulation believers as to when the rapture takes place. Some believe the rapture takes place at Revelation 6:12-17, others at Revelation 11:15-17, and others at Revelation 14:1-4. This inconsistency provides a major weakness for the mid-tribbers.

3.   Post-Tribulation Rapture

The post-tribulationists believe the rapture and the second coming to be one event. The rapture takes place at the end of the tribulation at the second coming of Jesus Christ to this earth. Believers go up to meet Jesus Christ in the air and come directly back with him to earth. Here the church will go through the Great Tribulation and be raptured at the very end. Since the rapture and the second coming are events that are one and the same, the tribulation could be imminent but the rapture cannot be imminent. This is an interesting concept. As a pre-trib believer, I could not agree with the first part of that statement. If I were a post-trib believer, it would be easy to agree with that statement. I agree, as a pre-trib, that the rapture is imminent.

There are a few places in the post-tribulation view that provide bold and glaring weakness. One is in Revelation, Chapter 19. This is an account of the second coming of Christ yet there is no mention of a resurrection or a rapture found here. The rapture is a major part of the post-tribulation view. Why would it not be included in Chapter 19?

Second, another weakness of this view is that God waits until the very end of the tribulation to pour out his wrath. This is just not what the scripture teaches. The wrath of God begins with the beginning of the seven year tribulation period. The first four seals are part of the first 3 ½ years of the tribulation. Sorrow and heartache, trouble and judgment begin during this time. Judgment intensifies with the beginning of the second 3 ½ years of the tribulation. God does not wait until the very end to pour out his judgment.

The third issue is a common sense issue. Why would God rapture the church up to meet him in the air and then return directly to earth? God does not even take the church on to heaven before they return. In my judgment, this view does not make any sense and has very little scriptural support.

4. Partial Rapture

This view is the least popular view on the rapture. Whether a believer is raptured or not depends upon the believer's degree of obedience. Those believers who are devout and who are serving and watching and waiting for the Lord's return will be raptured before the tribulation. Other believers who may not be so devout may have to spend some time in the tribulation before they are raptured. This rapture cannot be based upon one's salvation. It seems this rapture is based upon works such as waiting and watching.

J. Dwight Pentecost gave a list of misunderstandings as reasons to oppose this view: [46]

A. The partial rapturist position is based on a misunderstanding of the value of the death of Christ as it frees the sinner from condemnation and renders him acceptable to God.

B. The partial rapturist must deny the New Testament teaching on "the unity" of the body of Christ. This is a powerful point in opposition to this view because of the teaching of unity in the scripture.

C. The partial rapturist must deny the completeness of the resurrection of the believers at the translation.

D. The partial rapturist confuses the scriptural teaching on rewards.

E. The partial rapturist confuses the distinction between law and grace.

F. The partial rapturist must deny the distinction between Israel and the church.

G. The partial rapturist must place a portion of the believing church in the tribulation period.

J. Dwight Pentecost in his book, *Things to Come*, provides a list of scriptures in which those who adhere to this view use to support his position.[47] In the interest of space, I am going to list these scriptures for further study:

   (1) Luke 21:36
   (2) Matthew 24:41-42
   (3) Hebrews 9:28
   (4) Philippians 3:11
   (5) 1 Corinthians 15:23
   (6) 2 Timothy 4:8
   (7) 1 Thessalonians 1:10

The partial naturists interpretation of these scriptures do not seem too consistent nor in harmony with true doctrine or true interpretation of these scriptures.

5.   Pre-Wrath Rapture

This fifth view of when the rapture will take place is just before God pours his wrath out upon the earth and that is about midway through the last 3 ½ years of the Great Tribulation. They believe that is when God's wrath will start in Israel. This view put the beginning of wrath near the end of the tribulation's seven year period. This is not a very popular view. Scripture will not hold up this view. I believe the wrath of God begins at the very beginning of the tribulation. I believe the pattern of God used here will be one of increased frequency and intensity throughout the seven years of tribulation and will be the most horrible time known to man in all of history.

6.   Amillennialism

I felt a need to include this view because in this view, no rapture takes place. This view also teaches that there will be no 1,000 year reign of Jesus Christ on earth. This view holds that there is a kingdom on earth at the present time. It holds the kingdom of Jesus Christ is not of this world but rather is in the "hearts" of people on earth. The end of the world will take place when Christ returns and a general resurrection and a general judgment of all people on earth will take place. There are more who hold to this view than we may imagine especially in the Roman Catholic Church. There is little support for this view in the bible.

So when does the rapture take place?

1. Pre-Tribulation

As I have said earlier, I am a pre-tribulation believer. I believe that believers, the church, the "bride of Christ," will be raptured to meet Jesus in the air and will not go through any part of the seven years of tribulation (Revelation 3:10; 1 Thessalonians 1:10). There is an abundance of scripture to support this. This is the view that provides that "blessed hope" that I am so looking forward to. And when that Great Tribulation is taking place on earth, I am going to be in heaven with Jesus and so many others I love dearly.

2. Mid-Tribulation

God's wrath takes place during the second 3 ½ years of the tribulation. Believers will not have to go through God's wrath during this time.

3. Post-Tribulation

The wrath of God takes place at the very end of the tribulation. Only unbelievers will experience the wrath of God.

4. Partial Rapture

Believers will be raptured at different times. Some may even experience part of the tribulation. This is the weakest of all view of the rapture.

5.   Pre-Wrath Tribulation

The wrath of God will begin about half way through the second 3 ½ years of the tribulation. Believers will be raptured before the wrath begins.

Any serious bible student needs to understand these views and the degree to which the scripture supports each of them.

Bride of Christ

On Sunday evening, February 12, 2012, my pastor started the evening service in an unusual and quite unique way. He asked all who had cell phones to take them out of their pockets so they could make a contribution to the service. He gave a phone number to use to text to him the completion of the following statement. The statement was *The Church is _____. What and who is the church?* He had an extended screen to receive the responses. He read each response as they were delivered to him. There were many. The answers were quite interesting and also quite varied. I am not sure we heard a correct answer to what and who is the church. I have listed a few examples of the responses:

1.   It's a place where we worship.
2.   It's a place where we go on Sundays.
3.   It's a place where we can go and rest.
4.   It's a place where we go and worship with people.

There were over 100 responses submitted. As a teacher, I'm not sure that I heard any response that I would grade as an "A." Some of the responses were close but I never heard the comment that the church is the "bride of Christ." I never heard that the church is all saved believers from Pentecost to the rapture. The thought crossed my mind that maybe we are not doing a good job teaching basic doctrine.

However you approach what and who the church is, I believe you must start with the two following statements: (1) The church is the "bride of Christ" and (2) The church is all saved believers from Pentecost to the rapture. So the Church Age starts on the day of Pentecost and ends with the rapture of the church. The rapture takes place before the tribulation period which lasts for seven years. See the second chapter of Acts for the beginning of the church. [48]

1 And when the day of Pentecost was fully come, they were all with one accord in one place. 2 And suddenly there came a sound from heaven as a rushing mighty wind, and it filled all the house where they were sitting. 3 And there appeared unto them cloven tongues like as of fire, and it sat upon each of them. 4 And they were all filled with the Holy Ghost, and began to speak with other tongues, as the spirit gave them utterance......12 And they were all amazed and were in doubt, saying one to another, what meaneth this? 13 Others mocking said, these men are full of new wine.

Peter preached the first sermon at Pentecost.

14 But Peter, standing up with the eleven, lifted up his voice, and said unto them, ye men of Judaea, and all you that dwell at Jerusalem, be this known unto you, and hearken to my words: 15 For these are not drunken, as ye suppose, seeing it is but the third hour of the day. 16 But this is that which was spoken by the prophet Joel. 37 Now when they heard this (Peter's sermon), they were pricked in their heart, and said unto Peter and to the rest of the apostles, men and brethren, what shall we do? 38 Then Peter said unto them, repent, and be baptized every one of you in the name of Jesus Christ for the remission of sins and ye shall receive the gift of the Holy Ghost..... 41 Then they that gladly received his word were baptized; and the same day there were added unto them about three thousand souls.

So the church begins with these 3,000 individuals. It includes all Jews and gentiles who truly know Jesus Christ as their savior. Those who have had their sins forgiven because of what Jesus did at Calvary. Those who have accepted the shed blood of Jesus Christ on Calvary as an atonement for their sins. This group from Pentecost to the rapture is known as the "bride of Christ." There could not even be a church until Jesus went to Calvary and shed his blood. In doing this, Christ Jesus purchased the church and that church became his bride.

I am teaching the book of Revelation on Wednesday nights at my church. As I write this, we are nearing the end of the book but it has taken us about two years to get this far. As we have gone through this awesome book, I have tried to emphasize the significance of becoming a true believer during the Church Age. Because you have become a saved true believer during the Church Age also means you are a member of the "bride of Christ." It means that not everybody will get to be a member of the "bride of Christ." For example, Old Testament saints will not be members of the "bride of Christ." Once the church, bride of Christ, is raptured to heaven the marriage of the "bride" to the "bridegroom" who is Jesus Christ, will take place. Then the bride will be where Jesus is. They will be with Jesus for the seven year period in heaven. During this seven year period when the church is in heaven, the tribulation is taking place on earth. Then the bride will return with Jesus to earth when Jesus stops the Battle of Armageddon. Neither Jesus nor his bride ever returns to the third heaven.

One Tuesday morning after bible study, an older lady approached me and said "Dr. Lindsey, may I tell you something?" I said "yes mamm, you may." She said "I don't agree with you that once we are on earth with Jesus Christ that we will never return to the third heaven. Once Jesus stops Armageddon, we will return to heaven." I told her if she could show me in the bible where we return to heaven, I will surely take a strong look at it. She never did. The thought that struck me was that we do a poor job of teaching scripture. I believe and agree that we are not thorough enough in our teaching and thus we are poor students of the bible.

After a 75 day period, Jesus sets up his millennial kingdom on earth. He will rule and reign with his bride from the millennial temple with King David as his regent. This ruling and reigning with Jesus will last for a 1,000 years. The significant truth is that if you are truly saved you will be with Jesus for all the rest of eternity and all those others who are saved and whom you love dearly.

So in defining the church, we must distinguish this group of saved believers from Pentecost to the rapture. We must also distinguish this group as the "bride of Christ." We will be unbelievably blessed because we are a member of this group. Not all saints will be members of this group as the "bride of Christ." What a unique blessing this is to always be a member of this select group forever.

1 Thessalonians 4:13-18

When anyone wants to know more or reach a higher level of understanding about the rapture, they turn to 1 Thessalonians, Chapter 4: 13-18. Also, included in this search for more understanding about the rapture is 1 Corinthians 15: 51-53. Add to these versus John 14: 2-3.

Paul wrote this first epistle in response to some of the questions the people were having in Thessalonica. His desire was to instruct them further and hopefully give these believers some comfort regarding the concerns troubling them. One of the major concerns was that some of their people, perhaps family, had died since he was there. They wanted to know when they would see their loved ones again. Paul told them exactly what would happen when the rapture takes place. Paul explained to them that when the rapture happens, their loved ones will be resurrected and will be "caught up" to meet the Lord in the air. At that same moment, they will follow their loved ones and together they will be raptured up to meet Jesus in the air. He gave them a step-by-step account of what will happen when the rapture takes place (see 1 Thessalonians 4:13-18).

> *13 But I would not have you to be ignorant, brethren, concerning them which are asleep, that ye sorrow not, even as others which have no hope.*

> *14 For if we believe that Jesus died and rose again, even so them also which sleep in Jesus will God bring with him.*

15 For this we say unto you by the word of the Lord, that we which are alive and remain unto the coming of the Lord shall not prevent them which are asleep.

16 For the Lord himself shall descend from heaven with a shout, with the voice of the archangel, and with the trump of God: and the dead in Christ shall rise first:

17 Then we which are alive and remain shall be caught up together with them in the clouds, to meet the Lord in the air: and so shall we ever be with the Lord. Wherefore comfort one another with these words. [49]

Step One

Understanding regarding their loved ones who had died and whom they loved dearly. Paul was telling them to "sorrow not" because you will see them again at the rapture.

Step Two

If we believe that Jesus died and rose again, then we must believe that when Jesus returns in the clouds, he will have your dear loved ones with him. He will bring the souls and spirit with him to be joined with that body that was placed in the grave and that body will be changed into a new resurrected body that will go up to meet Jesus in the air (See On The Resurrected Body).

Step Three

Your dear loved ones who have died will go up to meet Jesus in the air first. We who are alive will in no way prevent this from happening.

Step Four

When the Lord descends from heaven, he will descend with a shout, with a loud voice, with the trump of God calling your dead believing loved ones from the grave and they shall rise first.

Step Five

Then those who are alive when that happens will be changed in "the twinkling of an eye" and will be caught up with their loved ones to meet Jesus in the air. And then we all will be with Jesus for all the rest of eternity. All these steps will take place instantly, in a moment, in the "twinkling of an eye." I believe the rapture is very near. Hallelujah!

Many contemporary scholars and writers believe the rapture to be soon and maybe sooner than we think. We must remember the rapture takes place before the seven years of tribulation starts. When I was younger, I wondered who the antichrist would be. I kept up with world news to see if there was a very strong personality emerging who might be the antichrist. I still keep up with what is going on in the world but now I know the antichrist will probably not appear on the scene before the tribulation starts. I, along with all other church age believers, will be in heaven when he comes on the scene. Thank you, Lord.

I have a friend who has tested my patience about the interpretation of this account of the rapture. Verse 17 of this account says that "then we which are alive and remain shall be caught up together with them in the clouds to meet the Lord in the air and so shall we ever be with the Lord. This verse indicates there will be a large number of saved believers who will never die. The phrase "which are alive and remain shall be caught up together with them," has bothered him greatly. He has asked me what I am going to do with Hebrews 9:27, which says "and as it is appointed unto man once to die, but after this the judgment.[50] I learned a long time ago that arguing never solved anything. Jesus taught us that we should fight our battles with scripture. With his word, Jesus confronted Satan with scripture. So if my friend would look a little above at verses 15-17, and also 1 Corinthians 15: 51-52 he would learn that physical death for the saved believer is not inevitable. If Jesus comes soon, I may be in that large number that "we which are alive and remain" (verse 17) will be "caught up together with them." There are many who believe they will be alive when Jesus comes for the church. Lehman Strauss who is a pre-tribulation literalist said that he believed he would be living when Christ returns. I know there would be conflict and confusion on every hand and in so many ways it would be difficult to address the state this world will be in. I do not believe God will continue to allow people to hate and murder the Jews, destroy Jerusalem (his chosen city and capital of the world someday), destroy his country, Israel, and persecute Christians all over the world. We who love the Lord claim Titus 2:13. We are:

> *Looking for that "blessed hope." And the glorious appearing of the great God and our Savior, Jesus Christ.*

Transformation of the Saints

In John, Chapter 14, verses 1-3, Jesus is telling his troubled disciples that he is going to come back for them.[51]

> *1 Let not your heart be troubled: ye believe in God, believe also in me. 2 In my Father's house are many mansions: if it were not so, I would have told you. I go to prepare a place for you. 3 And if I go and prepare a place for you, I will come again and receive you unto myself; that where I am, there ye may be also.*

In these verses, there are four very important points that need to be emphasized:

1. "Ye believe in God, believe also in me." He was telling his disciples that he was God. If you believe in God, you should believe in me also because I am God. This is similar to another verse where he told the disciples *"you have seen me, you have seen the father."* [52]

2. In these versus, he also told the disciples *"in my Father's house are many mansions."* These mansions are already in his father's house. At this point, Jesus has not gone anywhere. He is telling his disciples that he is going away to prepare a place for them.

3. *"I go to prepare a place for you."* Here he is telling the disciples he is going away and he is going to prepare a place for them. I know I am going to get some opposition here but I believe he is going away to prepare NEW JERUSALEM for them. He has been working on New Jerusalem for 2,000 years. I believe that New Jerusalem is sitting, at this moment, in the third heaven waiting for its role in eternity. Do I believe that Jesus Christ has been using a hammer and nails for the past 2,000 years building this beautiful city? No! I believe he could just speak it into being. What an awesome city. Look at Revelation, Chapter 21, to get just a glimpse of the beauty of this city. I certainly believe that Jesus is the overseer of this beautiful city where "his bride" will dwell for all eternity. There are no words in the English language that can describe how absolutely beautiful the city, New Jerusalem, is and will be. This point is a promise from God and God cannot lie. We can absolutely, 100%, count on the fulfillment of this promise.

4. In this point, Jesus is promising his disciples that he is going to come back to get them and take them to where he is.

When Jesus comes back for the church (all saved believers from Pentecost to the rapture) this event will be the greatest, most major event to ever take place in the history of mankind. There are some who cannot comprehend that all saved believers will come out of graves, out of the bottom of oceans, out of the bottom of rivers, out of mausoleums, from mountains and hillsides, and those previously cremated now being reunited with their spirits Jesus is bringing back with him when he returns for the church. All of this will happen in an instant, in the "twinkling of an eye." Someone has measured this to be in 11/100th of a second. Can you imagine being near a cemetery when this happens? At the moment when the spirit will be united with its body and that body will be changed into its resurrected, immortal state. At the same time, those who are not "dead in Christ" but alive will be changed in an instant into a new, resurrected, immortal body. Both will be given a new beautiful "white robe" and will be caught up to meet Jesus in the air. Jesus will carry them to New Jerusalem. What a reunion that will be!

First just to see Jesus will be so awesome. To see him face-to-face. To thank him for Calvary and all the other blessings he has given us across the space of our lives on earth. And then to see mom, dad, brothers, sisters, and other kin who are part of that reunion. I had the sweetest mother and father-in-law and they will be part of that reunion. My father-in-law and I may get together and sing. He had such a great bass voice and he loved to sing. There are others I sang with here or earth. I am looking forward to seeing them again.

Occupants of New Jerusalem

Some writers try to portray the message that everybody on earth will have residence in the city, New Jerusalem. That is simply not the case. After studying many different writers, you can come away more confused than when you started. We should all stay as close to scripture as possible which is the best we can do. There are a few scriptures that make this topic comfortable and not so confusing.

If we believe that New Jerusalem is ready and waiting for us in the third heaven, and I believe that it is, then the first to occupy the city will be those in the rapture. That will be the church, the bride of Christ. The church will include all saved believers from Pentecost to the rapture. So the church is one group who will reside in that city. New Jerusalem will be the eternal abode of the church. In John 14:3, Jesus is telling his disciples that *"where I am he shall be also."* The church is the bride of Christ and the "bride" will be with Jesus for all the rest of eternity. No scripture indicates any other permanent residence for the "bride of Christ."

Some believe the rapture will include Old Testament saints. This cannot be true. First, the rapture includes the church and there was no church in the Old Testament. The church had its beginning in Acts, Chapter 2. The church was a new entity in the program of God. Second, when the rapture takes place, the "dead in Christ will rise first." There was no "dead in Christ" of the Old Testament saints. Christ had not come to this earth thus he had not died on the cross in the Old Testament. John Walvoord, one of the most respected bible scholars of our era, says that "old testament saints will be raised from the dead after the great tribulation at the second coming of Christ." [53] He says there is no passage in scripture which teaches that Old Testament saints will be raised at the time the church is raptured which is before the final tribulation. So the Old Testament saints will be raised from the dead during a 75 day period between the ending of the seven years tribulation and the beginning of the millennium.

Another group that will be raised from the dead between the ending of the tribulation and the beginning of the millennium are those who are saved during the tribulation. These individuals will be martyred because of their refusal to worship the world ruler or the antichrist. Revelation 20:4-6 refers to the resurrection of this group of believers:[54]

4 I saw thrones on which were seated those who had been given authority to judge: and I saw the souls of them that were beheaded for the witness of Jesus, and for the word of God, and which had not worshipped the beast, neither his image, neither had received his mark upon their foreheads, or in their hands: and they lived and reigned with Christ a thousand years. 5 but the rest of the dead lived not again until the thousand years were finished. This is the first resurrection. 6 Blessed and holy is he that hath part in the first resurrection: on such the second death hath no power, but they shall be priests of God and of Christ, and shall reign with him a thousand years.

Walvood says this resurrection will occur before the millennium and after the second coming. It follows Christ's return (Revelation 19:11-21). He says probably several days after the second coming and not before it nor at the time of his second coming. This resurrection is to a physical life just as the Old Testament saints is to a physical life.

The Old Testament saints as well as the tribulation martyrs will be given new resurrected and glorified bodies at their resurrection. The Old Testament and tribulation martyrs will be raised at about the same time. So these two groups with "the bride of Christ," who have already received their new resurrected and glorified bodies when the rapture took place, will rule and reign with Christ forever. These three groups are now fit to go into God's earthly kingdom and what three groups they are. Can you imagine associating with these people along with Jesus Christ for all the rest of eternity? This time will never end.

As stated early the "bride of Christ" will be the first to occupy the city, New Jerusalem. Remember "the bride of Christ" includes all saved believers from Pentecost to the rapture. I believe the city, New Jerusalem, will hang in space over Israel during the thousand year millennium. During this time, New Jerusalem will be the abode of the bride of Christ. The saints will have their new resurrected and glorified bodies. No sin can enter New Jerusalem. Our new bodies will be sinless. Secondly, when Old Testament saints and martyred saints are resurrected by Jesus Christ during that 75 day period between the end of the tribulation and the beginning of God's kingdom on earth, those saints will take up residence in New Jerusalem. They will have newly resurrected, glorified, and sinless bodies. New Jerusalem will be the eternal abode of these three groups. God, himself, will have residence in New Jerusalem along with Jesus Christ. He will rule and reign from the new millennial temple in Jerusalem. These groups will travel from New Jerusalem to earthly Jerusalem at will. Remember they will travel at the speed of thought. J. Dwight Pentecost makes a very interesting statement in his book *Things to Come*. He says that "this city seems to take her chief characterization from the bride who dwells there." [55] That is to say that New Jerusalem gets its distinguishing and unique character from the bride of Christ.

Consequences of the Rapture

Several writers have given thought to what this world will look like after the rapture has taken place (Hitchcock, Hagee, Russell, and others). I do not find this thought as being fully developed. I also believe this thought to be serious with far reaching consequences. I doubt the thought of what this world will look like after the rapture will be fully developed in this book. I do believe this reality deserves more serious consideration and a more in depth study by writers of prophecy. A look at what is going to happen here on this earth when the rapture takes place is going to be awesome and quite chaotic.

As I have become older, I have become more anxious about height. I can get too high very quickly. My wife and I drive to Michigan every few years to visit some of my family. My wife is a good driver and she drives a lot when we travel. A few years ago, we were in the car and I never shall forget when we crossed the bridge in Cincinnati, Ohio. It was late one afternoon (about shift change) and it was raining. When you are up on top of the bridge if you look to your right, you can see over into the Cincinnati Reds baseball team stadium. There were six lanes of traffic going both ways, bumper-to bumper, and driving speeds of 60 plus miles per hour. Mixed in with all those cars were many 18 wheeler trucks. The thought struck me, what if the rapture took place at this moment? Can you imagine the chaos and death that would take place? Many of the drivers of those cars and trucks (including my car) will have Christian drivers who will be snatched out of those cars and trucks and raptured to meet Jesus in the air. What will happen to the car we are driving? What will happen to all those cars and trucks? That will be the largest pile-up this world has ever known. Many of the cars and trucks will be falling off the edge of that bridge. Many of those who are not Christians will be killed or maimed. This will not just be happening on that bridge in Cincinnati, Ohio... it will be happening all over the world. How many people will be killed all over the world when the rapture takes place? What will happen to the on-going functioning societies on earth? What will happen tomorrow at those companies and factories and all the other places where these people work.... including those who were raptured as well as those who were killed? Others may not be able to get to their jobs because of streets and highways being impassable with all forms of debris including steel and human bodies. Many companies will not be able to function because many of their top executives were taken in the rapture. Again, this will be a worldwide phenomenon. Yes, the world will be left in a mess when the rapture takes place. No one will plan for this event. It will happen without warning. The rapture is a "sign less" event. Jesus will appear in the clouds and the voice of the archangel will summon the dead in Christ from their graves and they will go up to meet Jesus in the air.

Have you ever thought about being near a cemetery when the rapture takes place? There is a song that says "Something's Going on in the Grave Yard." That "something" is going to be those saved believers coming up out of those graves and they are going up to meet Jesus in the air. Marble mausoleums will topple and release those saved believers so they can meet Jesus in the air. There are saved believers who have died and their remains are in the bottom of oceans and rivers. There are those who have been burned to death in fires. Many have been cremated and their ashes have been scattered in the oceans, on hillsides, and on other landmarks. Some individuals have been placed in urns and are in homes as an honor to their memory. Regardless of where the individual is placed upon their death, that final resting place is considered their grave. There are some who have asked the question "Can the Lord Jesus collect the saved believers from oceans, rivers, marble mausoleums, or burned ashes wherever they may be?" The answer is yes and he will. When the voice of the archangel sounds calling forth the saved believers from Pentecost to the rapture, they will come forth, be given new bodies, and go up to meet Jesus in the air. Hallelujah!

There are about 93,000 airplane flights in the world each day. Whenever the rapture takes place, there will be many pilots who will be taken in mid-flight. Many of the passengers will also be taken. For those on those planes who are not saved, it will be a terrifying time. The plane will crash to the ground. For the passengers it will be certain death. Where will these planes crash on earth? Some, no doubt, will crash into large cities and others in residential areas causing many deaths.

Many homes will be left empty. Mine will be. Maybe food will be left on the stove…almost ready to serve. The supper dishes will be left in place on the table. Some individuals in the home will just vanish while others may be left. Some may have just gathered to share a meal and then suddenly vanish leaving nothing behind but the clothes they had been wearing. Someone may be in the shower.….the water left running when they are part of those called in the rapture. A doctor may be in the middle of surgery when suddenly taken along with several of the nurses who were assisting. Two may be standing carrying on a conversation when one vanishes mid-sentence. The confusion will be great.

I believe one of the most difficult situations the rapture will create will be in relationships. People will be trying to locate their missing loved ones. They will be calling everywhere only to find the telephone lines are either jammed or destroyed. There will be two in bed and then one is no longer there. There will be two in the kitchen having coffee and then one realizes that only the clothes and coffee cup remain where the other individual was sitting. I believe another extremely difficult situation would be for a mother to go to the bassinet to get her baby and find the baby gone or she begins looking for other young children and they cannot be located. This will be a very sad moment.

It will be very interesting as to what the headlines will be in the next morning's paper (if there is one). You can be sure the secular humanists will have every explanation they can think of to explain what happened to possibly a billion plus people who are now missing from the earth. CNN will have a heyday. The scriptures teach that all of this will take place in "the twinkling of an eye."

The rapture is not without examples in the bible.

1. Genesis 5:21-24

21 And Enoch lived sixty and five years, and begat Methuselah
22 And Enoch walked with God after he begat Methuselah three

hundred years, and begat sons and daughters 23 And all the days of Enoch were three hundred sixty and five years 24 And Enoch walked with God: and he was not; for God took him.

In this passage, Enoch was walking with God and God suddenly took him to heaven. Enoch never experiences a physical death. In the rapture of the church, there will be a group that will not taste a physical death (1 Thessalonians 4:17). In Hebrews 11:5, we find another verse that tells us that Enoch was taken without seeing a physical death. It says by faith Enoch was translated that he should not see death; and was not found, because God had translated him: for before his translation he had this testimony, that he pleased God. [56]

2. 2 Kings 2:11

And it came to pass, as they still went on, and talked, that, behold, there appeared a chariot of fire, and horses of fire, and parted them both asunder; and Elijah went up by a whirlwind into heaven.

In this verse, we are told about the translation of Elijah. Elijah did not see a physical death. He was taken to heaven in a chariot of fire by a whirlwind. We also see here the power of God at work. We must remember that "our ways are our ways" but "his ways are his ways" and we must place our faith and trust in his ways, always. There is a third example that I must include and that is the rapture of Jesus when he ascended back to the father in heaven.

3. Acts 1:8-11

8 But ye shall receive power, after that the Holy Ghost is come upon you: and ye shall be witnesses unto me both in Jerusalem, and in all Judaea, and in Samaria, and unto the uttermost part of the earth. 9 And when he had spoken these things, while they beheld, he was taken up; and a cloud received him out of their sight. 10 And while they looked steadfastly toward heaven as he went up, behold, two men stood by them in white apparel; 11 which also said "ye men of Galilee, why stand ye gazing up into heaven? This same Jesus, which is taken up from you into heaven, shall so come in like manner as ye have seen him go into heaven.

In all three of these examples, the person was taken into heaven by God where he resides. You see, the natural body has to be transformed because it is not fit to live in heaven. The body is sinful and sin cannot enter the gates of heaven. God cannot abide where there is sin. Transformation means "to change into another form" "to change or move from one condition to another. [57] When we are raptured into heaven we are transformed or we are given a new body; one without sin. There we have witnesses to the transformation of both Elijah and Jesus. When Jesus was transformed (moved from heaven to earth), his disciples watched as he ascended into heaven (Acts 1:9). Elijah's rapture was witnessed by Elisha.

Earlier, I stated the rapture takes place before the beginning of the seven years tribulation period. There is plenty of scriptural support for this theory. Luke 21:36 states:

36 Watch ye therefore, and pray always, that ye may be accounted worthy to escape all these things that shall come to pass, and to stand before the son of man. [58]

Other verses supporting a pre-tribulation rapture include:

1. 1 Thessalonians 1:10….*"which delivered us from the wrath to come."* [59]
2. Revelation 3:10…*"I also will keep thee from the hour of temptation, which shall come upon all the world….*[60]
3. 1 Thessalonians 5:9 *"For God hath not appointed us to wrath……*[61]
4. Romans 5:9…*"we shall be saved from wrath through him."* [62]

5. John 14:3...*"and if I go and prepare a place for you, I will come again, and receive you unto myself, that where I am, there ye may be also."* [63]

There are many other verses that give support for a pre-tribulation rapture. None give any stronger support than from Grant Jeffrey who found an old manuscript. I loved the writings of Grant Jeffrey. We are going to miss him. I take this from John Hagee, *From Daniel to Doomsday.* [64] Grant Jeffrey has completely debunked the notion that the early church did not believe in a pre-tribulation rapture. He discovered an old manuscript from A.D. 373 in which Ephraem the Syrian wrote "For (at the rapture) all the saints and elect of God are gathered, prior to the tribulation that is to come, and are taken to the Lord lest they see the confusion that is to overwhelm the world because of our sins."

When the rapture takes place, this world will be in a state of destruction, disorganization, confusion, and chaos. People all over the world will be in a state of dismay and anxiety. This earth has been in a state of war since the Korean War in the early 1950's. The world has to be war weary. There are major events in our immediate future. They tell us that the next major event on God's prophetic calendar is the rapture. I agree. There are those who will tell you that "I have heard all of my life that the rapture will take place soon and that Jesus is coming soon." That is true and I have heard it also. The bible tells us that in the end times there will be scoffers and unbelievers. In the book of II Peter 3 verses 3 and 4 it says 3 *Knowing this first, that there shall come in the last days scoffers, walking after their own lust* 4 *and saying, where is the promise of his coming? For since the father's fell asleep, all things continue as they were from the beginning of the creation.* [65] But, there are some things that obviously these people who say these things are not aware of. Some things have to be in place before Jesus returns that were not in place at the time of the Korean War. Such as:

1. Israel was not a sovereign state until 1948.
2. The Jews were scattered all over the world until 1948 when they begin to return to their homeland. Today, there are about seven million Jews who have returned to Israel.

3. There has to be a re-gathering of the Jews to their homeland.

4. Israel has fought six wars since it became a nation. None any more important than the "six day" war. The Jews had to have complete control of the "dome of the rock." Someday, the third temple will be built there.

5. The "six day war" established more definite boundaries for Israel.

6. Jerusalem is the capital of Israel. Someday, Jerusalem will be the capital of the world.

Before 1948, none of these things were in existence. The scoffers still exist today. They will just not believe. But please believe me, Jesus is coming back soon to rapture his church to be where he is. That is a promise. Review John 14-2-3. [66]

2 In my father's house are many mansions: if it were not so, I would have told you. I go to prepare a place for you 3 And if I go and prepare a place for you, I will come again, and receive you unto myself; that where I am, there ye may be also.

These things are in place now and we would do well to watch because there is good reason to believe his coming is near. I believe the bible teaches this.

I believe the rapture is near and as I stated before, the rapture will leave the world in a very chaotic condition. The worse the world has ever seen. No doubt the tribulation will be worse. There are those who believe the rapture will take place at other times (mid-trib, post-trib). I have provided strong evidence for the pre-trib position. I believe the condition of the world will be conducive for someone coming on the scene and putting things back together. That is exactly what is going to play into the hands of Russia.

There are three events that writers try to determine when they will take place. There are certainly different views as to when they will occur. For example, there is strong scriptural evidence that the rapture will take place before the seven year tribulation. However, not everyone agrees with this (mid-trib and post-trib). The amillennialists do not even believe there will be a rapture. There are different views as to when the Ezekiel 38 and 39 war will take place. One very popular writer believes this war will initiate the last three and a half years of the tribulation. I believe there is strong evidence against that position. This event will be discussed later. There are also different opinions about when the Psalm 83 war will take place.

The following scenario seems to me to be a very logical order of these events with scriptural support. Not all other writers would agree with this placement. Nor would I necessarily agree with all of their views. The easiest of all is the placement of the rapture before the tribulation period. There is such strong evidence for this placement. The evidence has been provided earlier. I believe the Ezekiel 38 and 39 war will take place sometime after the rapture and before the tribulation starts. The main reason I take this view is because it would give Israel seven years to burn the weapons left behind by the invading force of the enemy. We do not know how much time will be between the rapture and the beginning of the tribulation but we need seven years before the end of the tribulation to burn the military hardware of the enemy. There are two reasons this seven year period is important. First, the burning of the military hardware is needed because one third of the trees will be destroyed at the first trumpet judgment. Second, seven years is needed for the cleaning of the land of all the dead bodies (seven months) and all the military hardware. If this view is correct, just look at how close we may be to the rapture. Several prophecy scholars take this view. Others do not agree with it.

I believe the Psalm 83 war takes place before the tribulation starts. Maybe even before the rapture. Refer to Psalm 83:4 [67] *They have said, come, and let us cut them off from being a nation; that the name of Israel may be no more in remembrance.* This is the very language that we are hearing from Muslim nations today, especially Iran. Iran's president, Ahmadinejad, has used almost the exact words of Psalm 83. Israel is surrounded by Muslim nations today. All of them would love to see Israel removed from that land. The Ezekiel 38 and 39 war will be designed to do just that but it will fail. It will be led by Russia and Iran. I will discuss this war later.

So the rapture is the next thing on God's prophetic calendar. I believe that it is and I also believe it is near. When Jesus Christ comes back in the clouds and calls the church, his bride, to meet him in the air, he will then lead the saints back to heaven to be with him forever. I believe the saints will be taken back to New Jerusalem which will be their home forever. I believe this because in John 14:2-3 [68] Jesus says *I go to prepare a place for you. And if I go and prepare a place for you, I will come again, and receive you unto myself; that where I am, there ye may be also.* This has to be New Jerusalem. When he came to earth the first time, he came from where God is, the "third heaven." There is not a lot of information on the third heaven; however, the entire Chapter of Revelation 21 is devoted to New Jerusalem. It is absolutely going to be a gorgeous and a beautiful city to live in for the rest of eternity. How absolutely wonderful it will be! You may wonder if that city will be large enough for all the saints to live in. It will be. As beautiful as the city is going to be, I have always thought that it will be the relationships that will be what makes it truly beautiful. The main reason is that Jesus will be there and he will be there forever. Can you imagine being with Jesus for the rest of eternity? Jesus will make the city beautiful because:

1. He is the one who went to Calvary.
2. He is the one who loved us so much that he died for us.
3. He is the one who suffered and shed his blood at cruel Calvary.
4. He is the one who looked down from that cross as he was dying and was concerned for his mother's care.
5. He is the one who provided salvation for us by his death.
6. He is the one who asked his father to forgive the soldiers who nailed him to the cross.
7. He is the one who rose from the dead and lives today.
8. He is the one the grave could not hold.
9. He is the one I have sang praises to all of my life.

10. He is the one who knows about the tears I have shed and how I worshipped long after midnight while trying to get home from an appointment.
11. He is the one who has heard my voice as I have told him about my love for him before going to sleep each night.
12. He is the one who will make it possible for me to be able to see my sweet and loving parents again.
13. He is the one who will make it possible for me to see my loving brothers and sisters again.
14. He is the one who will make it possible for me to see some of my loving friends who I worked with while traveling to sing gospel music. How I long to see them.
15. He is the one who will make it possible for me to see a loving nephew that was like a brother to me.
16. He is the one who will wipe away all tears from our eyes.
17. He is the one who will wipe away all sorrow and sadness.

There is a host of other reasons why the New Jerusalem will be so beautiful and certainly its physical beauty will be overwhelming. But again, the main reason that New Jerusalem will be so beautiful is because <u>Jesus will be there</u> and the saints will rule and reign with him for all of eternity. Also, we can say that God himself will be there. I know that Jesus told his disciples that "I and my father are one." He also told his disciples that "if you have seen me you have seen the father." [69] I will admit that I do not understand all of this but I know when we get to New Jerusalem where Jesus will lead us after the rapture takes place, it will be truly awesome. Hallelujah!

God does not leave us without knowledge of our new home, New Jerusalem. This is going to be our new home for the rest of eternity. It will be the eternal abode of "the bride of Christ." We will live there in our new bodies. New Jerusalem is a real place. Its dimensions and physical nature are given in Revelation, Chapter 21. I will have a mansion there. I won't just be wandering around New Jerusalem without a definite place. I will have a definite address. I believe "the bride of Christ" will live in their new home, New Jerusalem, for seven years while the seven year of tribulation is taking place on earth. Later, I will discuss the seven years in New Jerusalem and the seven years of tribulation.

With the help of the Holy Spirit and with great excitement, I want to discuss the nature and beauty of our new home:

1. The city is going to be the same width, length, and height. The dimensions will be equal. The city will be about 1,500 miles wide, 1,500 miles long, and 1,500 miles high. That is a huge city! The city's walls will be about 216 feet high and are usually referred to as jasper walls. The measurements seem to indicate the city is a cube. There are those who believe the city to be a pyramid. Dr. Harry Ironside and Clarence Larkin who are highly respected prophecy scholars see the city as a pyramid (see the city illustration as a pyramid drawn by Clarence Larkin).

2. Each wall will have three gates. There will be twelve gates to the city. An angel will be at each gate. Just above each gate one of the names of the twelve tribes of Israel will be written. It seems to me, the pyramid will be the most logical shape of the city. This is because the pyramid would place less stress on the foundation than if the city were in the shape of a cube. The builder of this city is the carpenter from Nazareth and he certainly knows better than I do. There are three gates on each side (north, south, east, and west). Each gate is a pearl.

3. The city also has twelve foundations and inscribed in each foundation are the names of the twelve apostles of Jesus. Surely, Judas will not be one of the twelve names inscribed. It is my belief that Paul replaced Judas in becoming the twelfth apostle. Some believe Matthias succeeded Judas; some believe it was Paul. You never hear the name of Matthias being mentioned again. But just look at all Paul did. Paul wrote half of the bible. If indeed it was Paul, then his name will be inscribed on one of the foundations.

4. The city will be of pure gold (this pure gold will be like clear glass). All twelve foundations will be a different precious stone.

Precious stones today carry great value. All precious stones are considered beautiful, expensive, exalted, and some of the most cherished items known to man. The stones are of different and varied hues and tents blended together to provide the most beautiful cluster of colors.

A. Jasper

This diamond is crystal clear. It is said that the walls of the city will be made of jasper. This clear crystal may have a tent of yellow, red, and brown making it the most beautiful jasper color eyes could ever behold.

B. Sapphire

The color of this precious stone is blue. This stone is mentioned in Exodus 24:10 as the foundation of God... ."And there was under his feet as it were a paved work of a sapphire stone, and as it were the body of heaven in his clearness." It is also mentioned in Exodus 28:18; Revelation 21:10; Ezekiel 1:26; 10:1

C. Chalcedony

This stone is greenish in color. It is mentioned in Revelation 21:19.

D. Emerald

This stone is green in color. It is mentioned in Exodus 28:18; 39:11; Revelation 4:3; 21:19.

E. Sardonyx

This stone is red in color. Robertson describes it as white with layers of red. (McGeep. 1072)

F. Sardius

This stone is fiery red in color. It is mentioned in Exodus 28:17; Ezekiel 28:13; Revelation 21:20.

G. Chrysolyte
This stone is golden yellow in color with a golden hue. It is mentioned in Revelation 21:20.

H. Beryl
This stone is green in color with a sea green tent. It is mentioned in Revelation 21:20.

I. Topaz
This stone is greenish yellow in color with a golden greenish tent. It is mentioned in Exodus 28:17 and Revelation 21:20.

J. Chrysoprasus
This stone is golden-green in color and has been described as sea green. It is mentioned in Revelation 21:20.

K. Jacinth
This stone is violet in color. It is mentioned in Revelation 9:17; 21:20.

L. Amethyst
This stone is purple in color.

As I have said before, I believe that New Jerusalem is sitting in the third heaven waiting for its place, position, and role in the future and eternity. This will be the home of saved believers from Pentecost to the rapture. It is going to be the most beautiful and breathtaking sight you can imagine. We have never seen anything as beautiful as our eternal home. Can you imagine the blend of the precious stones I have just described as is found in Revelation, Chapter 21? New Jerusalem will truly light up the universe. Our life is going to be so pleasant, peaceful, happy, and loving in our new home. Hallelujah! Come, Lord Jesus!

Chapter 4

SEVEN YEARS IN HEAVEN

Some time ago, a lady after bible study came up to me and said "Dr. Lindsey, I need to talk to you." I said okay, how can I help you? She said "I don't agree with you that when we come back with Jesus to stop Armageddon that we will never return back to the third heaven." I said, well, it is true, we will never go back. We just spent seven years there. If you can show me in the scripture where we do go back to the third heaven, I will certainly take a look at that scripture. I never heard from her again. When we are raptured we are taken to New Jerusalem.

The seven years we spend in New Jerusalem is not without activity. Although the bible does not give us a lot of information about what we will be doing, we will be involved in a few major activities. The Bema Judgment, the marriage of the Lamb, the marriage supper of the Lamb, and certainly there will be worship of the Lamb. There will also be a lot of time for fellowship with so many loved ones who are there. I believe one of the very first events to take place when we get to heave will be the "Bema Judgment."

A. The Bema Judgment

Often times you see this referred to as the judgment seat of Christ. This is no doubt the first event that will take place when we get to heaven. This is not a judgment to determine whether we are saved or not. We are saved or we would not be there. When we are saved on this earth, we are to serve Jesus until we die or the rapture takes place. Actually the "bema" seat came from the sports world where the referee or judge would sit on a raised platform and judge those who were playing and at the end would reward those for how well they played. So here, Jesus is the judge sitting on the "bema seat" judging each person for how well they served him while here on earth whether good or bad. I believe the Bema Judgment will be one of the first events to take place because heaven will be the most pure and true place possible. What do I mean? I mean I believe there may be some Christians in heaven who may believe they will be rewarded for some deeds that may be judged to be wood, hay, or stubble. Their motives for doing those deeds were just not true and sound. When Jesus Christ gets through with the "Bema Judgment," the rewards given to Christians will be the most pure, fair, and truly earned possible. When this judgment gets rid of the deeds of wood, hay, and stubble, just look at what "Heaven "will be like. It will be true and pure and that is the reason the "Bema Judgment" is no doubt the first major event to take place when we get to heaven.

The concept of motivation is very important in this process of determining whether a deed is good or bad and should receive a reward. Rewards are tested by fire to see if they are gold, silver, and precious stone or whether they are wood, hay, or stubble. If the reward is wood, hay, or stubble, they will be burned up in the fire and the individual will suffer loss. If the reward is gold, silver, or precious stone, and purified in the fire, the believer is rewarded because these rewards have eternal value and he will hear those precious *words "well done, thy good and faithful servant: thou hast been faithful over a few things, I will make thee ruler over many: enter thou into the joy of the Lord."* [70] The person who does all he can because he will be seen by others and his motive is to do things because of the rewards he will receive is doing those things for the wrong motive. His rewards are likely to be burned up as wood, hay, and stubble. His reward has no lasting value. His motive is wrong. The individual who does all he can for the Lord Jesus Christ while he is on this earth because he loves the Lord Jesus has his motive right. He serves the Lord Jesus on this earth because he loves him. His motive is right and his reward has eternal value.

God did not give all believers a lot of talents. Nor did he give the same believers the same talents. He gave different believers different talents. I have been teaching prophecy for a long time. When this topic comes up, there is obvious concern. I teach when a person gets saved he is supposed to start serving Jesus using the talents he has been given. All of us have something that we can do for the Lord. There is a man in our church that does not sing in the choir, does not preach, does not teach but he is responsible for making sure the offering is taken up every service. That means there are men going down every aisle, counting the number of people in each pew, and then returning the money and count to him. That is a big job. He is so faithful. He will be rewarded for his faithfulness because everyone at church has confidence in him and the job he does. There is another man who passed away a couple of years ago. This man took up the offering in that same aisle for as long as I knew him. There is a lady who does not sing in the choir, who does not teach, but she is so faithful. She is always making others happy. She always has a smile and she is always in her pew. She gives out love and everybody loves her. These are talents these people have and I believe they will be rewarded by Jesus at the "Bema Judgment." Mark Hitchcock says in his book, *The End*, that "The Lord will find something in the life of every believer to praise and reward. [71] I have heard it said that what we do here on earth serving the Lord Jesus is practice for what we will be doing in heaven.

There are generally five rewards throughout the New Testament. Remember, the Bema Judgment is not to determine a person's salvation. An individual is saved or they would not be at this judgment. These five rewards given as crowns are found in James 1:12, Revelation 2:10, 2 Timothy 4:8, 1 Thessalonians 2:19, 1 Peter 5:4, 1 Thessalonians 2:19, Philippians 4:1, and 1 Corinthians 9:25.

I believe all saints will receive at least one of these crowns. Some saints will receive more than one crown for their service to Jesus Christ when they were on earth. This event will not be one of sadness and jealousy. When a saint sees another saint receiving more than one crown, they will feel love, joy, and happiness. At the appointed time when Jesus Christ is sitting on his throne, all these crowns will be placed at the feet of Jesus. This is because he is the one to be honored. He is the holy one. He is the one who is to receive praise. He is the one the saints will shout glory to the Lamb. He is the one who went to Calvary and shed his blood for us. He is our savior. He is the one who the saints will scream "thank you, Lord Jesus." This will be the greatest event any saint has ever experienced.

This event will not be an unorganized and haphazard event. It will be organized and everyone will be so full of joy and happiness they won't ever want it to end. We must remember praising him will last for all the rest of eternity. Hallelujah! Thank you, Lord Jesus. The order in which these crowns are given is not found in literature. Perhaps, because different saints will be receiving different crowns. The following are the five crowns that will be given:

1. A Crown of Life (James 1:12, Revelation 2:10)
   This Crown of Life refers to the saved, the true believer, who when he is tested by the trials of life applies the word of God to fight these trials. Christians will be tested many, many times. These tests will provide many opportunities for the Christian to put his faith in God's word to help him win the test. We are tempted so many times. Jesus Christ was tempted by Satan. Jesus Christ used scripture to fight his battles with Satan. He always won the test. Look at the martyrs of the tribulation period. They truly endured to the end. They were obedient to the end and it cost them their lives. They will receive the "Crown of Life" at the Bema Judgment.

71

2. The Crown of Righteousness (2 Timothy 4:8)
   All believers can be rewarded with this crown. This crown refers to those righteous deeds such as gold, silver, and precious stones and has been tested in the fire. These are righteous deeds that truly define the Christian. The Christian that truly loves the Lord Jesus and looks for his return. Hallelujah! They are Christians who look forward to living for all the rest of eternity with the Lord Jesus Christ.

3. The Crown of Glory (1 Peter 5:4)
   This is the crown that will be given to those elders, pastors, teaches, and leaders who are willing to graciously and faithfully shepherd the flock. They fully oversee, and take care of God's people. They faithfully serve him and they will be given a "Crown of Glory." (Hebrews 2:9)

4. The Crown of Rejoicing (1 Thessalonians 2:19, Philippians 4:1)
   This crown is set aside for those who witness and win and lead others to Christ. I think some Christians may be surprised at how many times they may have had a part in someone else's decision to accept Christ. Many of us have witnessed to others. How many of these may have accepted Christ because of our witnessing? Those who are persistent in watching over other Christians such as Sunday school teachers, singers, etc.

5. The Incorruptible or Victor's Crown (1 Corinthians 9:24-27)
   This crown is given to those who practice self-discipline, self-control, and who overcome yielding to worldly behavior that would cause the Christian to deviate from the path that Christ prescribes for all Christians. This would be difficult without that daily walk with Jesus

Christ. When we are about to yield to temptation just look up to the cross.

Will we wear these crowns? Some saints will be given more than one crown and we can only wear one crown at a time. We will not wear these crowns. When Jesus gets through with the judgment of each and every saint, he will move from the judgment seat to his throne.

B. The Throne

This event will truly be awesome. I have said before I believe when the rapture takes place we will be taken to New Jerusalem. That is going to be the abode of the church. The home of the bride of the Lamb. Jesus told his disciples in Revelation Chapter 14-2-3:

> *"2 I go to prepare a place for you. 3 And if I go and prepare a place for you, I will come again, and receive you unto myself; that where I am, there ye may be also."*

So we will be taken by Jesus in the rapture to our new home which is the New Jerusalem in heaven. Nothing is described in the third heaven as being heaven. But just look at how much time and space is devoted to New Jerusalem being our eternal home. Why would Jesus need to go back to prepare a place for us if from where he came was where we would be taken when the rapture takes place? Why would the entire chapter of Revelation 21 be devoted to the beauty of New Jerusalem? Why would verse 9 call New Jerusalem the Lamb's wife?

There are millions of crowns given to saints at the Bema Judgment for the deeds they did for Jesus Christ while they were on earth. Now they are ready to place those crows at the feet of Jesus. In Revelation Chapter 4, verse 2, John saw *"a throne set in heaven, and one set on the throne."* That had to be Jesus. Psalm 11:4 says ..."*the Lord's throne is in heaven."*

The throne is a huge chair. The throne is a symbol of royalty. It is also a symbol of government. It is the place where the king sits and governs and makes judgment. Here the throne applies to the royal authority of God. At this time, God has given his royal authority to Jesus. Jesus and the father share the throne. Remember, the saints will share authority and government with Jesus. I would envision that chair to be raised and made with gold, silver, and precious stones. The seat may be purple because purple represents royalty. The throne sits at the base of a high wall made with some of the most beautiful material. There would be a large door directly behind the throne. This is where those who sit in that chair enter and exit. I can see twelve chairs on either side of the throne. At this event, there are twelve elders on each side of the throne where Jesus sits. Up over on the huge wall behind these chairs may be written on one side "The Twelve Tribes of Israel." On the other side, it may be written "The Twelve Apostles." This writing is made with a mix of gold and silver and trimmed with beautiful stones. I am not good at making something look beautiful but this throne will be the most beautiful thing you have even seen. It will truly be fit for a king.

At this event, the 24 elders who are sitting on either side of Jesus and the millions of saints will place their crowns at the feet of Jesus. If you have ever wondered where those crowns would be placed, now you know.

C. Worship

It is difficult to separate a discussion of the throne and worship because this event is definitely a time of worship. The only one at this event worthy to receive these crows is the Lord Jesus. He is one sitting on the throne and we are going to lay our crowns at his feet. Revelation 4:9-11 says: [72]

> *"9 And when those beasts give glory and honor and thanks to him that sat on the throne, who liveth forever and ever 10 The four*

and twenty elders fall down before him that sat on the throne and worship him that livith forever and ever, and, cast their crowns before the throne, saying 11 thou art worthy, Oh Lord, to receive glory, and honor, and power: for thou hast created all things, and for the pleasure they are and were created."

These verses provide us with the first great worship scene in heaven. The scripture gives us some indication about the nature of worship in heaven. In verse 10, the 24 elders "fall down before him that sat on the throne and worship him. Revelation 7:10-11 says: [73]

"10 And cried with a loud voice, saying, salvation to our God which sitteth upon the throne, and unto the lamb. 11 And all the angles stood round about the throne, and about the elders and the four beasts, and fell before the throne on their faces, and worshipped God."

We have never been to a worship service like this worship service. Verse 11 says the elders fell on their faces and worshipped God. When we lay our crowns at the feet of Jesus who is sitting on the throne and look upon his face and realize we are looking into the face of the one who died on that cruel cross of Calvary that will be enough to cause us to fall on our faces prostrate before him and worship him. We will praise him, honor him, and thank him for taking our place at Calvary. Because he did, I have a savior. His name is KING JESUS. I believe there will be many, many opportunities to worship him. Those worship services will truly be awesome. You won't have to beg anybody to "please let me sing in the choir." Everybody will be on pitch and you will never hear any singing more beautiful. I believe there will be a variety of singing in heaven. The singing in heaven will certainly never be boring. We will praise him with singing for all the rest of eternity. Glory to the Lamb. Praise his name. Saints are looking forward to worship in heaven. My favorite musical instruments have always been the piano and the trumpet. You have never heard anything as beautiful as these two instruments playing "How Great Thou Art." Those playing these instruments will be the best and Jesus will be there. We will spend a lot of time in heaven in worship. Worship in heaven will be awesome and beyond description. I am looking forward to worship in heaven and being able to worship my savior, the Lord Jesus Christ. I am one of those who believes it will be soon. Come, Lord Jesus.

Some time ago, I was at the church I attend. It was a Monday and as I walked by the sanctuary the doors were open so I could see inside. I could see all the way to the altar. I saw my pastor and two other men (who are ministers on our church staff), lying prostrate on the floor of the alter with their faces down. They were praying. I thought what a humble, sincere, and awesome way to worship. They were truly honoring and worshipping the Lord Jesus Christ. They often start the week by praying and praising the Lord Jesus. These men were not trying to impress anyone because other than Jesus Christ they were the only ones there.

D. Fellowship

One of the most often asked questions is "Will I know my family and my loved ones when I get to heaven?" The answer is a great big YES. In answering this question, we can draw from the scripture in 1 Corinthians 13:12 which says *"For now we see through a glass, darkly; but then face to face: now I know in part; but then shall I know even as also I am known."*[74] To me, that verse is not difficult to interpret. It simply means people will know me as they knew me on earth. I will know others as I knew them on earth. I know there will not be marriages in heaven but I believe I will know my wife as a very special person. I do not believe you can live with someone for over 53 years (at the time of this writing) and that person not be someone very special to you in heaven. We will not be married to each other in heaven but we will be very special to each other. I cannot believe God will make something less special in heaven than what it was on earth. I actually believe our relationship will be greater and even more special in heaven. My wife and I have a son and daughter who are also very special to us here on earth.

I have been wondering where in this writing would be a good place to reveal another experience that my wife and I experienced. I have shared this with several people and they all agree with me that it should be included. My wife and I always wanted to have two children. Our son was born first and after about three or four years, we decided it was time to have a second child. I was in school at the University of Mississippi and my wife began having trouble with the pregnancy. We decided she should stay home in Muscle Shoals, Alabama so she would be close to her doctor. I received a call about midnight one night and was told my wife had lost the baby and I needed to come home. It was suggested I wait until morning to travel but I disagreed and left for home. The drive home was difficult. It was very foggy and I was driving too fast because I wanted to get home as quickly as possible. On one stretch of the road in the deep fog, I came upon a group of about 8-10 deer standing in my lane. When they saw the headlights, they decided to shuffle to the right side of the road. One of the deer decided she wanted to go to the other side of the road and that put her directly in my lane. I hit and killed the deer. She went right over my car and created quite a scare for me. I backed up and pulled her to the edge of the road and continued home. Needless to say, I drove at a slower speed the rest of the way. My wife was in the hospital so I drove directly there. She was doing okay other than the fact she had just lost the baby. When I told my family of the incident with the deer, one sweet lady said "Well, you dumb man. Why didn't you put the deer in the trunk and bring it home with you?" I told her I did not want to take the time because my wife was in the hospital and I did not know her condition. I wanted to get to her as soon as possible.

As I mentioned earlier, this baby would have been our second child. My wife was a few weeks along in the pregnancy when she lost the baby. However, God did see fit to bless us with a beautiful daughter about three years later. She is a precious child. When our daughter was a senior, she competed and won the Miss University pageant at the university where I taught. She went on to compete in the Miss Alabama pageant that year as well.

The most important part about this entire story is about the baby we lost. You see, I believe my wife and I have three children. The son and daughter God gave us here on earth and the one that is in heaven. We do not know if that child is a son or daughter. At that time, the medical profession could not predetermine the gender of a child. I do not know how God will work this out but I believe when I get to heaven there will be a handsome young man or a beautiful young lady who will walk up to me and say "you are my daddy." We will embrace and declare our love for each other. My wife and I have three children. I do not know how God will handle things like this but I know it has already been worked out. It is part of his plan and it is greater than I can imagine right now. I just know I am looking forward to it. This event may not be so far away.

Either with the rapture or in physical death when we draw our last breath, we will be in the presence of the Lord (2 Corinthians 5:8). After we see the Lord Jesus Christ, we will see our loved ones (mom, dad, sons, daughters, brothers, sisters, others). So when I get to heaven I will see my other child. I know others who can tell this same story. And look at all those aborted babies. God has a plan. You and I are part of this plan because we are going to rule and reign with him. I may not look at my "three" children in heaven as sons and daughters but I know I will know them in a very special way. Our relationships will be exalted in heaven, not diminished. This will be true with all our family members in heaven.

We have all had friends and extended family members that we love and look forward to seeing again. Friends that we played sports with and went to school together. I sang in quartets all my life. I am so looking forward to seeing those friends again. The greatness of this is that we will have all eternity to fellowship together. I know I will get to sing with them again in heaven.

There will be many individuals that have touched our lives in so many different ways here on earth that we will get to spend eternity with in heaven. It may have been some teacher who helped you with those difficult math courses or a music teacher in high school. It may have been your favorite teacher in high school or your favorite professor in college or your major professor of coursework in your graduate program. It may have been some favorite pastor or some other person who led you to Christ. Do you know who baptized you? Do you remember who married you? It may have been some Sunday school teacher. Is there anyone whom you may have told "I am glad you came my way on this earth?" I'm happy there have been a few who have touched my life in a very special way. I look forward to seeing them and being part of their fellowship. Remember, there will not be any hate in heaven. Everybody will love everybody and there will not be anyone you dislike. Jesus Christ is going to rule and reign in heaven and we are going to rule and reign with him. Remember in heaven, we will have our new body and our new body will not have the capacity to hate. In our new body, we will not have the capacity to sin. Can you imagine living with Jesus Christ and a host of others that you love and are looking forward to spending a lot of time with in fellowship? In heaven, there will not be any hate, sin, deception, hurt, sorrow, anxiety, dread, wait, arguing, fussing, dislike, murder, or politics (Jesus will rule). There will be no disappointment (I don't like the way you did that), or self promotion (I have more riches than you so I am better than you). Our heavenly father owns it all and we are his children. There will be no war and fighting among the nations. Remember, you and I will be ruling and reigning with King Jesus and with David as our Regent. There will be peace, joy, happiness, love, care, and this will never end. It will last for all eternity. There will be no doctors, lawyers, hospitals, disease, or police. With the beginning of the millennium, this earth will become what God intended in the Garden of Eden. The curse will be lifted and this earth will undergo much change. Major changes will occur in the worlds of agriculture, medicine, and animal. In the agricultural world, there will be plenty. There will not be any hunger. In the medical world, people will begin to live much longer because there will not be all of the serious medical problems like cancer, heart disease, diabetes, and many others that kill so many today. The animal world will no longer be a carnivorous world. The education world will undergo radical change. Jesus, himself, will be the superintendent of education. I believe there will be teaching and learning beginning with the start of the millennium. Someone has said that we are serving an apprenticeship here on earth for what we will be doing in heaven. I agree. Read Ephesians, Chapter 4, especially verses 8 and 11. So there is scriptural support for learning and training in heaven. The bible will be our main textbook and in our textbook you will not find all the garbage you find in textbooks today.

When we get saved, we are supposed to serve Jesus Christ here on earth. He has given each one of us at least one gift and maybe more. To many people he has given more than one gift. We are supposed to use our gifts. To some, he gave to rule over one city. To some, he gave to rule over five cities, and to some he gave to rule over ten cities. Some of this ruling and reigning may take serving an apprenticeship here on earth in preparation for the ruling and reigning to come. So God is grooming us for leadership. He's watching to see how we demonstrate our faithfulness. He does that through his apprenticeship program, one that prepares us for heaven. Christ is not simply preparing a place for us; he is preparing us for that place. [75]

So you see, we will not be using all our time relaxing. We will be busy doing many other things. All these other things will not be a dread. Even the work will be fun and we will be happy. I tell my class that I teach on Wednesday nights that I am looking forward to taking my day in the hayfield. I also tell them my best buddy during the millennium is going to be a big fuzzy bear. His name will be "Whisel." Can you believe you will live in a world like this? You will because the curse will be lifted. Alcorn would say that our performance as we serve him on earth will determine how much he will put us in charge of in heaven. The person who is willing to humble himself and have a loving positive motive in serving him will be exalted in heaven. *"For everyone who exalts himself will be humbled and he who humbled himself will be exalted."* [76] If we serve faithfully on the present earth, God will give us permanent management positions on the new earth. I have been a teacher all of my life. I have often wondered if God had something to do with me being a teacher. I tend to believe he did. What we do on earth may be what we do in heaven. Since I have been a teacher on earth, it is likely I will be a teacher in heaven. I certainly believe there will be books, learning, and teaching in heaven. Ephesians, Chapter 4, tends to support preparation for future vocation.

Much of our fellowship will be as it was on earth. Loving others and enjoying the company of others as we carry out the assignments of Jesus Christ and King David. Much of our fellowship will be leisure time with so many whom we loved on this earth and with so many that we are looking forward to spending a lot of time with especially so many of the old testament saints. I think it would be wonderful if I could get to sing with some of those I sang with on earth. We have all eternity. I believe we could get around to that. I know many saints who love to sing. There are certainly many Old Testament saints I am looking forward to spending a lot of time with. Paul wrote 13 books of the bible. Wow! My Sunday school teacher wants to see Jesus, Paul, and his mother in that order. Paul is very high on my list. John and Daniel would not be very far behind.

E. The Marriage of the Lamb

The next major event to take place during those seven years in heaven and after the Bema Judgment is the marriage ceremony. The bridegroom is Jesus Christ. The bride is the church. The church includes every saved person from Pentecost to the rapture. The bride will include all those who were raptured to heaven. So the marriage takes place in heaven. It is truly mind boggling to realize that you were born between Pentecost and the rapture. You might ask why that is so important and exciting. The answer is because you have the opportunity to be a member of the bride of Christ if you accept Jesus Christ as your personal savior. Realizing that you will be a member of the "bride of Christ" for all eternity. Hallelujah!

This will be one of the most glorious events we will ever experience. I do not think this will be the first event to take place when we get to heaven. But it will happen soon after the Bema Judgment. Do you remember the time of your wedding? There will come a time when God will tell his son to "go get your bride." If you read 1 Thessalonians, Chapter 4, verses 13-18, you will learn about this event. In verses 16 and 17 of Chapter 4, Jesus will call the church, which is his bride, home. We will go up in the clouds to meet him. Millions will go up at this time. When we are in the clouds, the bride (the church) will see the most beautiful, perfect, glorious, powerful, humble, kind, and loving person ever seen. His presence is indescribable. Jesus Christ will take us home to New Jerusalem which is the home of the bride. Soon after we get there, a wedding ceremony will take place. Everybody will be wearing their best. The dress of both the bridegroom and the bride will be more than our eyes can behold. This is just the way heaven will be. You can read about our new home in Revelation, Chapter 21. Men, do you remember looking down that aisle and watching your beautiful bride walk down to the front of the church for the marriage ceremony? To you, she was the most beautiful bride on earth. Women, do you remember walking down that aisle looking at that handsome man you selected to be your bridegroom? Jesus Christ gave his life for his bride. This marriage ceremony will be the greatest event we have ever experienced maybe other than when we got saved and that event was pretty awesome.

F. The Marriage Supper of the Lamb

There has been much disagreement in the literature about where the marriage supper of the Lamb takes place. Some time ago, as I read the works of several contemporary writers and I started keeping a tally of those who believed the "marriage supper" would take place in heaven and those who believed the "marriage supper" would take place on earth during the millennium. At present, those who believe the "marriage supper" will take place in heaven outnumber those who believe it will take place on earth by a score of eight to three. These eleven writers are considered among our best prophecy scholars today. Some of these writers make no sense to me at all. This is important because your support for your belief may result in a loss of credibility. I know it has affected me this way. I try to understand their support for their position and it never seems to get explained. This is a weakness in a lot of writers. Be simplistic so readers will understand. We need to keep our readers and keep them hungry for prophecy. They sure do not get much of it from the pulpit because many of our pastors today will not spend the time and energy needed to make prophecy understandable. I believe prophecy can be made understandable, exciting, and will keep the reader hungry for more.

I am not sure I intended to say these things here but I guess it is because some explanations about the "marriage supper" I have read have been pitiful. I do not believe prophecy has to be difficult to understand. Be a literalist. Stay with what the Bible says. Do not try to make it mean what you want it to mean. The interpretation of where the "marriage supper of the Lamb" takes place is a good example of what I am saying. I am one of those eight who believe the marriage supper takes place in heaven. Why do I believe this? Because I believe that is what the bible teaches. All you have to do is look at Revelation, Chapter 19:7-9: [77]

> *7 Let us be glad and rejoice and give honor to him: for the marriage of the Lamb is come, and his wife hath made herself ready. 8 And*

to her was granted that she should be arrayed in fine linen, clean and white: for the fine linen is the righteousness of saints. 9 And he saith unto me, write: blessed are they which are called unto the marriage supper of the Lamb. And he saith unto me, these are the true sayings of God.

In verse 7, the time for the marriage has come. His wife (the church) hath made herself ready. In verse 8, the bride (the church) is dressed in fine linen, clean and white. This fine linen is the righteousness of saints. This is the dress of the bride. Now in verse 9, John writes *"Blessed are they which are called unto the marriage supper of the Lamb."* So the "marriage supper" takes place in heaven. They are still in heaven because verse 11 starts by saying *"And I saw heaven opened and behold a white horse; and he that sat upon him was called faithful and true, and in righteousness he doth judge and make war."* [78] Jesus Christ is still in heaven when this verse starts. The marriage supper has already taken place in verse 9. So the "marriage supper" takes place in heaven. That is what the scripture teaches.

There are several prophetic issues that have troubled writers and prophecy scholars and this is one of those issues. I include myself in this group. No one seems to be willing to step forward and provide a viable scripture based position on this issue. The following is a viable position and I believe it is based upon scripture. In ancient Israel, a marriage had to go through three stages. It seems to me that marriage in America may go through these same three stages.

Stage 1A: The Betrothal

A betrothal for marriage was a binding agreement in ancient Israel. It set the young bride apart for the young man. One could only get out of a betrothal by death or divorce. Remember, when Joseph discovered that Mary was pregnant he decided to divorce her secretly. Joseph did not carry out the divorce because he had a visit from an angel who convinced him the baby would be the Son of God.

Stage 1B

Remember that when we accept Jesus Christ as our savior we become a member of the "bride of Christ." This means that for contemporary western society we are spiritually "betrothed" to him. We, in western society, also become engaged. Most often by giving an engagement ring to the bride to be. This is not as binding in the western world as it was in ancient Israel. So there is a lot of similarity between Stage 1A and Stage 1B.

Stage 2A

The second stage in ancient Israel is the coming of the bridegroom to meet his bride. Remember marriages in ancient Israel were very often arranged and it was possible the bridegroom had not yet seen his bride. The bridegroom would go to the bride's house with a few friends and take her to his house that he had been preparing for them when the time of marriage arrived.

Stage 2B

This stage could be equivalent to stage 2A by Christ "coming in the air" to meet his bride. Christ is coming in the rapture for his bride. We may say that in contemporary western society the bridegroom has never seen the bride until they accept him as savior. That is the only way we in the western world or any other place can become a member of the bride. Thus a member of the bride has never seen the groom other than through the eyes of "His" word.

Stage 3A

In this third stage the "marriage supper" takes place. This is the celebration of the marriage and it took place in the home of the groom.

Stage 3B

The marriage celebration cannot take place until the rapture takes place and the bride is taken to her home which is New Jerusalem. Here the marriage has already taken place and we are at the marriage supper to celebrate the marriage. The most puzzling question for most scholars is who are the guests that will attend the celebration of the marriage supper. There is always a group of invited guests at most weddings. Revelation 19:9 *says "Blessed are those who are called to the marriage supper of the Lamb."* [79] So who are these guests? They are the souls of the Old Testament saints and the thief on the cross, and most tribulation martyrs. I believe these have substantive bodies. They do not have their resurrection bodies yet. They are already in heaven enjoying the presence of Christ. They are in an intermediate state and are the guests at the marriage supper and are in the presence of the assembled angelic host of heaven. The marriage supper will be the last major event that will take place during that seven year period in heaven. It will take place just before the return of Christ at the second coming. Many of these were the saints who were in paradise. Remember, paradise was a compartment of hell. The first thing Jesus did after he died was to go to paradise and clean it out and take all who were there to heaven with him when he ascended. So now paradise is in heaven. In the western world, a celebration takes place. A meal is provided for the invited guests and congratulations are offered by the invited guests. After this celebration, the married couple leaves for a short vacation and this begins their married life together.

The place of the marriage supper is definitely in heaven, the home of the bride [80] This marriage supper takes place in heaven as seen by John. [81] Grant Jeffrey is referencing John, Chapter 14, verses 2-3. He is right on and placing this in its proper perspective and supported by this scripture. When the rapture takes place, Jesus Christ will lead all the church age saints, his bride, straight back to New Jerusalem. Look at the scripture:

2 In my father's house are many mansions: if it were not so, I would have told you. I go to prepare a place for you. 3 And if I go and prepare a place for you, I will come again, and receive you unto myself; that where I am, there ye may be also.

There is not anything described to us in the scripture about the third heaven. We know that is where God is and it is from where Jesus came. Here Jesus is telling his disciples he is going away to prepare a place for them. And if I do this I am surely coming back to take you to that place I have prepared. I believe that New Jerusalem is sitting in the third heaven right now waiting for the rapture to take place. I am also going to live in a mansion. Look at verse 2. This is important. We are not going to be running around New Jerusalem not knowing where our mansion is located. In heaven, New Jerusalem, we are going to have an actual address.

A person in a group that I meet with once a month said a preacher we all know did not believe we would know each other in heaven. That means, if that is true, I will not know my neighbors until I am assigned my mansion and learn who lives around me. That hurt my feelings that a minister of the gospel would believe that. I do not agree with his theory at all. We will know Jesus Christ. When we draw our last breath here on earth, if we know him as our savior, we will be escorted to the presence of Jesus. In 2 Corinthians 5:8 it says *"to be absent from the body, and be present with the lord."*[82] So we will know the Lord Jesus first. Then I believe I will see my mother and father and other family members. Then I will see others that I loved so dearly here on earth. I believe there is much scriptural support for knowing others in heaven.

What about the transfiguration? They knew each other and had never seen each other before. There is a verse that says *"we will know as we are known."* [83] Yes, we will know each other. There are many people I am looking forward to seeing and being able to be with for eternity. I sang with some of these people and I believe I will have many opportunities to sing with them again in heaven. And I'm not leaving out some of those great piano players that we sang with. I believe this verse tells us that we will know so many of our friends by name. My Sunday school teacher says he wants to see Jesus Christ first. Then his mother. Then Paul. I agree with him except I would put my wife in that group. I have lived with her for over 52 years. I believe I will know her more and greater than I do here on earth. I know there will not be marriages in heaven but I believe she will be more special to me than others.

When I get to heaven, I will see my mansion. Jesus says in the father's house there are many mansions. Does this person believe we will not know others living in mansions around us? That is foolish. As I said earlier, I will have an address in New Jerusalem. I will know exactly where I live in heaven and I will learn exactly where others live. Remember, we will travel at the speed of thought. We can get to where others live quickly. Moses, Abraham, Paul, Peter, Daniel, Adam, Ester, Job, Matthew, and so many others. I will know where my wife lives. I hope her mansion is next door and that my children and grandchildren also live close by. Heaven would not be heaven if we did not know others who are there. If I die before the rapture, an angel will be right there to escort me to the presence of Jesus. Then I will see others in paradise who are there, even the thief on the cross. He is there. When I die or when the rapture takes place, is that the end of my knowing my wife? Is that the end of remembering that beautiful girl who walked down the aisle and said "I do"? The beautiful girl who finished her college degree and taught school for 32 years. That beautiful wife who bore our two children and lost one that we will see when we get to heaven. That beautiful wife who watched and helped as our son played football and baseball all the way through high school. That beautiful wife who watched and helped as our daughter was Miss University of North Alabama and competed in the Miss Alabama contest. That beautiful wife who stood by me as I had open heart surgery. That beautiful wife who watched and helped as we flew to Hawaii and drove to Texas, Michigan, Florida, and all the states in between. That beautiful wife who put up with my singing for all the years of our marriage (and still continues to do so). That beautiful wife who watched and helped as I worked through the Ph.D. program so I could teach at the university. All this and more and that person does not believe we will know each other in heaven? I believe I will get to know my wife in a grater and deeper way than I know her on earth. And do you know what shakes the very bones of my body? To realize that I will love her more in heaven than I do on earth. God will teach us how to really love each other. To realize I will be with Jesus Christ, my wife, our children, grandchildren, parents, brothers and sister, friends, and so many others shakes my very bones. To know we are going to live in a place John described in Chapter 21 of Revelation. Remember Jesus promised us a mansion and he cannot break a promise. Paul was allowed to look into heaven. When they ask him what he saw, he could not answer them. He said there are not words to describe it. Folks, that is our future if we know Jesus as our savior. It may be very soon. I believe it will be.

Chapter 5

THE SECOND COMING OF JESUS CHRIST (THE GLORIOUS APPEARING – JESUS RETURNS)

Remember, the coming of Christ is in two phases. The first phase is when the saints, living and dead, are raptured to meet Jesus in the air. That blessed hope (Titus 2:13). The second phase is the second coming when Christ comes back to earth. That glorious appearing (Titus 2:13). The saints have been in heaven with Jesus for seven years. Now they are returning with him to set up his millennial kingdom. The rapture is a sign-less event. Nothing else has to happen before the rapture can take place and there are no signs we have to identify as to when it will occur. The rapture could take place at any moment. There are many signs that indicate "the second coming" is near. These signs include:[84]

- Israel becoming a nation 1948.
- Israel's control of all of Jerusalem in 1967
- The regathering of the Jews to their homeland, Israel (this is occurring now…over one third or about eight million Jews are back in their homeland)
- Wars and rumors of wars
- Nation rising against nation
- Kingdom rising against kingdom

- Famines and pestilences
- Earthquakes and false prophets

Are we not seeing all of these things at the present time? There will also be an increase in knowledge, transportation, and communication. It is believed that 80% of all scientists who have ever lived are still living today. Knowledge today is doubling every 12 months. Encyclopedias are no longer being printed today because by the time they are printed, they are out of date. Mark Twain traveled to the Holy Land in 1866 and it took him three months to get there. Today, that same trip would take about 12 hours. Today, we can watch a war as it is being fought. The bible says that *"as it were in the days of Noah, so shall it be with the coming of the son of man."*[85] Genesis 6:11 *says "the earth also was corrupt before God, and the earth was filled with violence."*[86] Has there ever been a time you can remember when there was so much violence? All of these are signs that we are nearing the end when Jesus Christ will return to this earth with his bride and all the holy angels with him to set up his earthly millennial kingdom. I believe his return is near. Hallelujah!

Jewish leaders led the Jews to reject Jesus as their messiah and led them astray by placing blinders over their eyes so they could not see that Jesus was truly their messiah. They now know he was their messiah. Now at a time when they are about to be destroyed by the armies of the antichrist, they plead for their messiah to return and save them. So the Jewish leaders led the nation to reject the messiahship of Jesus. Now, the leaders will realize the national sin and lead the nation to the acceptance of Jesus as their messiah. For three days, the Jews will plead for Jesus to return and save them. This call is found in Hosea 6:1-3. This call begins the last three days before the second coming.

For the first two days, Israel will confess their national sin and plead for Jesus to come back and save them. Jesus had already promised to save all of Israel. On the third day, after two days of the Jews' pleas, Jesus comes back to save them. This is when Jesus comes back to earth to stop the fighting at Armageddon. Jesus will return to earth to defeat the antichrist and his armies. Look at this account of the Jews in Hosea 6:1-3:[87]

1 Come, and let us return unto the Lord: for he hath torn, and he will heal us; he hath smitten, and he will bind us up. 2 After two days will he revive us; on the third day, he will raise us up, and we shall live in his sight. 3 Then shall we know, if we follow on to know the Lord; his going forth is prepared as the morning; and he shall come unto us as the rain, as the latter and former rain unto the earth.

Don't you know there is going to be some more rejoicing going on among the Jews when they look up on that third day and see Jesus step through that open door of heaven riding a great white horse? They knew he had control and that he would save them from being annihilated by the antichrist and his armies. God has made a covenant with Israel. Look at Romans 11:27. In this verse, the salvation for Israel is guaranteed. Romans 11:25-27 states the following: [88]

25 For I would not, brethren, that ye should be ignorant of this mystery, lest ye should be wise in your own conceits; that blindness in part is happened to Israel, until the fullness of the gentiles be come in. 26 And so all Israel shall be saved; as it is written, there shall come out of Sion the deliverer, and shall turn away ungodliness from Jacob: 27 For this is my covenant unto them, when I shall take away their sins.

These verses teach us that God is going to take away the national sin of Israel. He is going to take away the blinders of Israel and "all Israel shall be saved."

One of the major reasons why the Jews rejected Jesus as their messiah is "peace." They were promised peace all across time but peace never came. They have been scattered, they have been killed, and they experienced the 70 AD event when the temple and Jerusalem was destroyed. For over 2,500 years, they have not seen peace. The bible, for the most part, was written by Jews. There are 66 books in the bible but the Jews have only recognized 39. So they have been hindered by realizing that peace can only come by one man. The man of Jesus Christ. The blinders are coming off and the Jews are going to realize that Jesus is their messiah and during the last three days, just before

Jesus appears, they are going to plead for him to come back and save them. And that is exactly what he is going to do. There will never be any peace until the prince of peace, even Jesus Christ, comes back and brings peace with him. Paul says in Ephesians 2:14 that "He is our peace." Thank you, Jesus.

The confusion of the national sin of Israel will last for the first two days of the last three days before Jesus returns. I was discussing this with a minister and he asked me "where did you get all of this?" I just told him to read Hosea 6:1-3.

To me, this is some of the most important scripture in all of the bible. This is the role of the Jews in the second coming of Christ. The confusion of Israel's national sin and all of Israel is saved. How awesome it is to know that Israel is ready to go into the millennium and King David will be the Vice Regent during the millennium. The actual words of this national confession by Israel of their sins is found in Isaiah 53:1-9: [89]

1 Who hath believed our report? And to whom is the arm of the Lord revealed? 2 For he shall grow up before him as a tender plant, and as a root out of a dry ground; he hath no form nor comeliness; and when we shall see him, there is no beauty that we should desire him. 3 He is despised and rejected of men; a man of sorrows, and acquainted with grief: and we hid as it were our faces from him; he was despised, and we esteemed him not. 4 Surely he hath borne our griefs, and carried our sorrows: yet we did esteem him stricken, smitten of God, and afflicted. 5 But he was wounded for our transgression, he was bruised for our iniquities; the chastisement of our peace was upon him; and with his stripes we are healed. 6 All we like sheep have gone astray; we have turned every one to his own way; and the Lord hath laid on him the iniquity of us all. 7 He was oppressed, and he was afflicted, yet he opened not his mouth: he is brought as a lamb to the slaughter, and as a sheep before her shearers is dumb, so he openeth not his mouth. 8 He was taken from prison and from judgment: and who shall declare his generation? For he was cut off out of the land of the living: for the transgression of my people was he stricken. 9 And he made his grave

*with the wicked, and with the rich in his death; because he had done
no violence, neither was any deceit in his mouth.*

No doubt most people believe the return of Jesus will be to the
Mount of Olives. Actually, his return will be to the city of Bozrah.
This is a city in southern Israel which is just across the border of a
place called Patra. Patra is a large place dug out of the mountains in
southern Jordan. This is a place the Jews fled to at the midpoint of
the tribulation when the antichrist went into the temple and declared
himself to be God. The Jews fled to every hiding place they could find.
One of these places was Patra. Here, they depended on protection and
care by the Lord Jesus Christ. At this point, the Jews had already asked
for forgiveness of their sins and pleaded for him to save them. That is
the reason why Jesus starts in Bozrah when he returns. There is a great
remnant of Jews in Patra the antichrist would love to kill.

There are at least four scriptures that would identify Bozrah as the
city of the return of Jesus Christ:

1. Isaiah 34:1-7
    *"...behold it shall come down upon Edom, and upon the people
    of my curse, to judgment....for Jehovah has a sacrifice in Bozrah,
    and a great slaughter in the land of Edom."* [90]

2. Isaiah 63:1-6
    *"Who is this that comes from Edom, with dyed garments from
    Bozrah? This that is glorious in his apparel, marching in the
    greatness of his strength?"* [91]

3. Habakkuk 3:3
    *"God came from Teman, and the holy one from Mount Paran.
    His glory covered the heavens, and the earth was full of his praise."*
    Teman and Mount Paran are both in the area of Bozrah." [92]

4. Micah 2:12-13\

> *"I will surely gather the remnant of Israel; I will put them together as the sheep of Bozrah, as a flock in the midst of their pasture..."*[93]

The last sign given for the return of Jesus Christ is found in Matthew 24:29-30: [94]

> *29 Immediately after the tribulation of those days shall the sun be darkened, and the moon shall not give her light and the stars fall from heaven, and the powers of the heavens shall be shaken: 30 And then shall appear the sign of the son of man in heaven: and then shall all the tribes of the earth mourn, and they shall see the son of man coming in the clouds of heaven with power and great glory. 31 And he shall send his angels with a great sound of a trumpet, and they shall gather together his elect from the four winds, from one end of heaven to the other."*

Just after the ending of those tribulation days, we see the last sign of the coming of the Lord Jesus Christ. When the sun and moon stop giving their light and the stars fall from heaven. The earth will be in total darkness. Then suddenly Jesus Christ will break through this darkness. He will be riding a great white horse. John says in Revelation 19: [95]

> *"And I saw the heavens open; and behold, a white horse and he that sat upon him was called Faithful and True; and in righteousness he does judge and make war: and his eyes are a flame of fire, and upon his head are many diadems...he is arrayed in a garment sprinkled with blood...and the armies which are in heaven followed him upon white horses, clothed in fine linen, white and pure. And out of his mouth proceeds a sharp sword that with it he should smite the nations: and he shall rule them with a rod of iron...And he has on his garment and on his thigh a name written, King of Kings, and Lord of Lords."*

Jesus Christ will certainly not come back secretly. He will not make it unknown or try to hide himself. When he returns, he will be highly visible to all people on earth. The people of the earth will mourn him. The nations on earth will be in turmoil and troubled. People will be terrified at what they see in the heavens. In Matthew 24:30, we see that his coming is on the clouds of heaven. Often, we see the travel of Jesus is with the clouds of heaven. When he ascended back to heaven, he was "taken up" and a "cloud received him." We are told in Acts 1:9-11 [96] that *"this Jesus, who was received up from you into heaven, shall so come in like manner as ye beheld him going into heaven."* This does not say Jesus will return to the same place. Only that he will return in like manner. Please note his travel on "the clouds of heaven" in other places in the scripture. Also, note that in Revelation 19:11-16, the use of the word "armies" is plural. Clearly, there are two armies that will return with him. One of these armies has to be the saints who were raptured seven years earlier and who have spent seven years in heaven with Jesus. The other army is identified in Matthew 16:27: [97]

> *"For the son of man shall come in the glory of his father with his angels; and then shall he render unto every man according to his deeds."*

Although both of these armies will return with Jesus, neither of them will do any fighting. I wore the uniform of the United States Army. Here, I will wear the uniform of saints who are the "Bride of Christ."

There are many who believe the first presence of Jesus Christ on earth when he returns will be on the Mount of Olives. I have been among this group. But with further study, I have come to realize that before Jesus sets his feet on the Mount of Olives, he has a job to do in southern Jordan in the city of Bozrah. Remember, at the midpoint of the seven years tribulation when the antichrist broke the peace covenant with Israel, an angel told the Jews to flee for their lives to hiding places in the mountains of Israel and southern Jordan. For three and a half years, God kept them just as he did for 40 years when Israel was in captivity in Egypt. There is a large remnant of Jews hiding and finding safety in the city of Bozrah in the land of Edom which is in southern Jordan. A large concentration of Jews and leaders of the Jews will have escaped to a place called Patra. Patra is a city cut out of the mountainside in Bozrah. The nations of the earth will be gathered there. Other than the fighting in Jerusalem, most of the major fighting will take place in Bozrah. The desire of the antichrist is to annihilate the Jews. There are several verses to support this claim that Jesus came first to Bozrah to save that large remnant of Jews hiding in Patra. The first verses are in Micah 2:12-13: [98]

> *12 I will surely assemble, O Jacob, all of you; I will surely gather the remnant of Israel; I will put them together as the sheep of Bozrah, as a flock in the midst of their pasture; they shall make great noise by reason of the multitude of men...and their king is passed on before them, and Jehovah at the head of them.*

In these verses, the remnant of Jews has engaged the armies of the antichrist and finally win this battle. There is a misconception about Armageddon. There are many battles of Armageddon. It is best referred to as the "campaign of Armageddon." The second passage is in Isaiah 34: 1-7: [99]

> *Come near, ye nations, to hear; and hearken, ye people: let the earth hear, and all that is therein; the world, and all things that come forth of it. For the indignation of the Lord is upon all nations, and his fury upon all their armies: he hath utterly destroyed them, he hath delivered them to the slaughter. Their slain also shall be cast out, and their stench shall come up out of their dead bodies, and the mountains shall be melted with their blood...for my sword has drunk its fill in heaven: behold, it shall come down upon Edom and upon the people of my curse, to judgment...for Jehovah has a sacrifice in Bozrah, and a great slaughter in the land of Edom.*

Here, Isaiah is calling all the nations and telling them that God has indignation against them and their armies. He tells them they are to be slaughtered by the Lord. Verse six of this passage tells us that in a vision Isaiah saw the exact spot where these nations and their armies would be slaughtered. That spot is in the city of Bozrah in the land of Edom in southern Jordan. This third passage is awesome in its support of the claim that Jesus will come first to Bozrah. Isaiah 63:1-4 states: [100]

> *1 Who is this that cometh from Edom, with dyed garments from Bozrah? This that is glorious in his apparel, traveling in the greatness of his strength? I that speak in righteousness, mighty to save. 2 Wherefore art thou red in thine apparel, and thy garments like him that treadeth in the winefat? 3 I have trodden the winepress alone; and of the people there was none with me: for I will tread them in mine anger, and trample them in my fury; and their blood shall be sprinkled upon my garments; and I will stain all my raiment. 4 For the day of vengeance is in mine heart, and the year of my redeemed is come.*

These verses tell us a lot about where the Lord Jesus has been and what he has been doing. Isaiah, who was in Israel, in his vision saw a blood-stained person approaching him from the east, from the land of Edom and the city of Bozrah. This person was Jesus. He had been in Bozrah fighting the armies of the antichrist. This accounts for the blood stain on his clothing. He says *"their blood shall be sprinkled upon my garments, and I will stain all my raiment.* Verse three tells us he was fighting alone. Although he had two great armies with him, the saints and a host of angels, he did all the fighting alone. The two armies never entered the fighting. The answer to the question "Who is this person?" is answered in Isaiah 63:1 [101] *"He was traveling in the greatness of his strength, I that speak in righteousness, mighty to save."* Here we see the messiah marching toward Israel and he is coming from the land of Edom and the City of Bozrah where he has been fighting the armies of the antichrist, thus the bloodstains on his clothing. He fought alone. He had to because there was none to help and he fought to save that remnant of Jews that had been hiding in Patra. They were about to be destroyed by the antichrist. His clothing was splattered with blood from the slaughter of the armies of the antichrist.

This fighting will continue back north to the east of Jerusalem to the Valley of Jehoshaphat. We know the final battle of the campaign of Armageddon is Jerusalem. Satan knows he is being defeated in these battles. So he believes if he can destroy Jerusalem, he can defeat Jesus Christ. He orders his armies to destroy Jerusalem. Zechariah 12:8-9 states: [102]

> *"8 in that day shall the Lord defend the inhabitants of Jerusalem;....9 and it shall come to pass in that day that I will seek to destroy all the nations that come against Jerusalem."*

But we see in this verse, Jesus Christ, comes just in time to shield those who live in Jerusalem from being destroyed by Satan and his armies.

The last battle, which will not truly be a battle, will be when all the nations of the earth gather in the Megiddo Valley for the purpose of defeating Jesus Christ. All the armies of the earth cannot defeat Jesus Christ. And before he sets his feet on the Mount of Olives, he looks down and says "It is done." With the breath of his mouth, the word in his mouth, he declares all the armies of the earth defeated. They all drop to the ground dead. The two mighty armies with Christ, the saints and the mighty host of angels, never helped Jesus fight. They only stayed out of his way and watch him do his work. What an awesome and mighty savior is the Lord Jesus Christ.

The discussion concerning the return of Jesus Christ to this earth (the second event) was greatly helped by Arnold G. Fruchtenbaum in his book, *The Footsteps of the Messiah*. Dr. Fruchtenbaum has a Th.M., Ph.D., and is considered one of the foremost authorities on the nation of Israel. He is a messianic Jewish believer.

"Then his feet shall stand in that day upon the Mount of Olives, which is before Jerusalem on the east. [103] The Mount of Olives is about ten miles northeast of Jerusalem. When this victory ascent takes place upon the Mount of Olives, several major events take place:

1. The ending of the Great Tribulation.

2. Revelation 16:17-21 tells us that *"a great voice out of the temple and from the throne"* says *"it is done."* [104]

3. When this happens there will be "lightnings, and voices, and thunders."

4. Also, *"there was a great earthquake, such as was not since there were men upon the earth, so great an earthquake, so mighty."* [105] This means that this was the greatest earthquake to ever take place.

5. Also, *"Jerusalem the great city was divided into three parts and cities of the nations fell."* [106] So the whole earth shook.

6. There will be "great hail, every stone about the weight 120 pounds, came down out of heaven upon men." [107]

One of the greatest events to take place is when Jesus plants his feet on the Mount of Olives. A great valley will be created when half the mount will move toward the north and half of it will move toward the south. This valley will be created running east and west. This valley will create a way of escape for the inhabitants of Jerusalem from the great earthquake. Thus ends the Great Tribulation. Read and study Revelation, Chapters 6-19.

Chapter 6

75 DAYS

There is a 75 day interval between the ending of the Great Tribulation and the beginning of the 1,000 year Messianic Age. This 75 day interval can be divided into two periods. One is a 30 day period of time added at the beginning of the 75 day interval. Another 45 day period is added to the 30 day period which totals the 75 day period. Jack VanImpe in his prophecy bible gives reasons for these two additional periods at the end of the Great Tribulation. The first additional 30 day period will be necessary for God's people to prepare themselves spiritually to rule and reign with Christ. The scripture teaches the saints will rule and reign with Jesus Christ. Secondly, one of the major events of the 75 day time period is the "judgment of nations." This event is to determine if the people are "qualified to enter his glorious kingdom for a 1,000 years." It is interesting to note that it may take 45 days to complete this judgment. This is no doubt one of the major events of this 75 day period. This group lived through the tribulation period of seven years. They will enter the kingdom in their natural bodies. Their purpose will be to populate the millennial kingdom. There are several events that will take place during this 75 day period. After much effort, I have found no writer who has placed these events in chronological order. From this, there seems to be few efforts that are most urgent. The following is a list of things that are most necessary:

A. The Cleansing of the Land

We must remember this fighting took place from one end of Israel to the other. This is about 200 miles. There would be dead bodies throughout the land of Israel. It seems to me this would be among the first things that should be attended to because of the stench from the bodies and the huge birds who are feeding on the remains. There may be some lingering hostilities and much military hardware still scattered across Israel that will have to be cleaned up. There may also be some lingering hostilities in other parts of the world. If that is the case, Jesus Christ will put an end to any conflict found anywhere in the world. Some military hardware may even be found throughout the world. It would need to be cleaned away and put to some other use. There will be no more war. The Prince of Peace has come to this earth and brought peace that will exist throughout the earth. It seems there has been war going on somewhere in the world as long as I can remember. How wonderful it will be to realize there is total peace in the world. When I began thinking about this 75 day period, I made a list of major events that would have to be attended to by the Lord Jesus Christ. These include the "resurrection of Old Testament saints," the resurrection of tribulation saints," and the judgment of nations." There are others that will be discussed later.

B. The Judgment of Nations

It seems the Judgment of Nations is part of cleansing the land in preparation for setting up the millennial kingdom. The use of the word "nations" must be clarified. This judgment does not mean that all the nations of the earth are gathered to be judged. The word "nations" translated means Gentiles. The actual basis for this judgment will be anti-Semitism or pro-Semitism. So this judgment is going to be based on how

Gentiles treated the Jews during the Great Tribulation. The Gentiles from every nation will be gathered for judgment in the Valley of Jehoshaphat. This is a valley east of Jerusalem. The Lord Jesus Christ is the one doing the judging. Arnold Frsechtenbaum says the judgment of all Gentiles will be divided into two camps: the pro-Semitic sheep camp or the anti-Semitic goat camp. [108] The judge will place the sheep on his right and the goats on his left. He will place the sheep on his right because they are the ones who did good deeds to "his brothers," the Jews. Any time you see the phrase "his brothers," he is making reference to the Jews. The Jews had to flee death and destruction during the second half of the seven year tribulation period. They had no means of sustaining themselves. These saved Gentiles, the sheep, took care of the Jews in any way they could without letting the forces of the antichrist know they were providing for the Jews. These Gentile believers provided the fleeing Jews with food, shelter, clothing, and other necessities at risk to themselves. They would have been killed if they had been caught treating the Jews in this compassionate manner. These Gentile believers will be allowed to go into the millennial kingdom by King Jesus. They were saved and they expressed this by taking care of the Jews during the Great Tribulation [109]

The goats will be placed by the judge on his left hand. They are anti-Semitic. They never provided the Jews with any help during the Great Tribulation. They treated the Jews in a negative and harsh way. They were not saved by grace and so they will not be allowed to enter the millennial kingdom. It is a sad commentary for the "goats" on the left. They will be thrown into eternal punishment. They provided no help for the Jews, the brothers of Jesus. They "drove them out of their land, divided up the land, and enslaved the Jews." [110] Isn't that what we are trying to do at the present time? At the time of this writing, our President and Secretary of State are there now trying to convince Israel to give land for peace. They are trying to give their country to the Palestinians. That county does not belong to the Palestinians. This is God's country. Our President has turned his back on Israel and it is not going to work. Our leaders have not studied their bible. In Genesis 12:3 it says *"and I will bless them that bless thee, and curse them that curseth thee: and in thee shall all families of the earth be blessed."* [111] It is stated in Amos, Chapter 9, 14-15: [112]

> *14 And I will bring again the captivity of my people of Israel, and they shall build the waste cities, and inhabit them; and they shall plant vineyards, and drink the wine thereof; they shall also make gardens, and eat the fruit of them. 15 And I will plant them upon their land, and they shall no more be pulled up out of their land which I have given them, saith the Lord thy God.*

What we are seeing is fulfillment of prophecy. There is an interesting paragraph at the end of the article "Judgment of The Nations," in the *Popular Encyclopedia of Bible Prophecy* by LaHaye and Hindson. The paragraph is worth including in this writing.

> Men are accountable to the Lord God for what they do with His truth and His people. Some people might think that God is not watching, but the scriptures reveal that God knows everything man does and says. Man will be rewarded or punished in accordance with the standard of God's truth. This holds true for the Gentiles who are alive during the Great Tribulation. They will stand before the King at his second coming, and they will either be welcomed into or excluded from the messianic kingdom. [113]

This article was written by Paul Benware. Some time ago, I felt that I would like to become directly attached to Israel and the Jewish people. The Jews are being persecuted and killed today just as they will be during the Great Tribulation. Read this paragraph and it makes you want to ask the question: How many Gentiles are reaching out to help the Jewish people? Benware says that "men are accountable to the Lord God for what they do with his truth and his people." [114] God is watching us. He knows everything we do; everything we say; everything we think. We will be rewarded or punished in accordance with his truth. Those Gentiles who reach out and help his brothers (the Jews) will be welcomed into the millennial kingdom. There are enemies all around who would like to kill all Jews. I have made that direct association with Israel and the Jewish people at the time of this writing. So the "Judgment of Nations" is one major event Jesus Christ will have to attend to during the 75 day period. It is difficult to find any chronological order of first resurrections. Paul says in Corinthians 15:23 the righteous will be resurrected....each in his own order. Arnold Fruchtenbaum in his book *The Footsteps of the Messiah* says that "all the righteous will not be resurrected at the same time, but rather in a definite sequential order. He places the first resurrections into five stages: [115]

1. Resurrection of Jesus
2. Resurrection of the church saints at the rapture
3. Resurrection of the two witnesses
4. Resurrection of the old testament saints
5. Resurrection of the tribulation saints

C. The Resurrection of Old Testament Saints

The Old Testament saints will be resurrected during the 75 day interval between the end of the tribulation and the beginning of the millennial kingdom. The Old Testament saints must be resurrected so they can reign with the Lord Jesus in his millennial kingdom (1,000 years). The verse that clearly explains this resurrection is Daniel 12:2:[116]

> *"And many of them that sleep in the dust of the earth shall awake, some to everlasting life, and some to shame and everlasting contempt."*

This short verse tells us that the dead bodies of the Old Testament people are still in the dust of the earth. There are two groups there. The righteous and the unrighteous. The righteous will be resurrected before the millennial kingdom starts. They will awake to everlasting life. They will rule and reign with Jesus Christ and will share in the blessings of the millennial kingdom. The unrighteous will be resurrected at the end of the millennial period (1,000 years). They will take part in the Great White Throne Judgment.

D. The Resurrection of Tribulation Martyrs

These saints are those who will be killed during the time of the Great Tribulation. Revelation 20:4 best describes the tribulation saints. [117]

> *"And I saw thrones, and they sat upon them, and judgment was given unto them: and I saw the souls of them that had been beheaded for the testimony of Jesus, and for the word of God, and such as worshipped not the beast, either his image, and received not the mark upon their forehead and upon their hand; and they lived, and reigned with Christ a thousand years."*

This group was beheaded because they were not willing to worship the antichrist; nor did they worship his image; nor did they take the mark of the beast. This group of saints will be resurrected during the 75 day period. The tribulation martyrs and Old Testament saints will probably be raised at about the same time during the 75 day period. This will leave only the wicked dead who will remain in their graves until the end of the 1,000 years, the end of the millennial kingdom. Revelation 20:11-15 is a sad scripture to read. There are those who do not believe in a literal hell. Why would we not believe in a literal hell if we believed in a literal heaven? Why would we believe in these literal resurrections and not believe in a literal hell? A literal death of Jesus Christ makes the difference. Jesus Christ was raised from the dead literally. Those who believe in this literally will live with him in a real literal heaven for all the rest of eternity. Heaven is a real place. Those who do not believe in a literal resurrection of Jesus Christ from the dead will be condemned to a literal hell that is a real place and they will be punished for all the rest of eternity. John described his vision: [118]

> *"11 Then I saw a great white throne and him who was seated on it. Earth and sky fled away; and there was found no place for them. 12 And I saw the dead, small and great, stand before God; and the books were opened: and another book as opened, which is the book of life: and the dead were judged out of those things which were written in the books, according to their works. 13 And the sea gave up the dead which were in it; and death and hell delivered up the dead which were in them: and they were judged every man according to their works. 14 And death and hell were cast into the lake of fire. This is the second death. 15 And whosever were not found written in the book of life were cast into the lake of fire."*

When we get saved, an angel writes our name down in the Book of Life. At the Great White Throne Judgment, the Book of Life is opened. Those whose names are not found written down in this book are thrown into the lake of fire. This is a literal hell fire where the antichrist, the false prophet, and Satan with his angels have already been thrown. Those who refuse Christ will experience eternal punishment. The greatest punishment in this is the eternal separation from God.

E. The Assignment of Responsibilities in the Millennial Kingdom

When I began to consider the events that would need to be covered during this 75 day period, I made a list of the obvious ones such as the resurrections of Old Testament saints, tribulation martyrs, and the Judgment of Nations. There are many other events but the assignment of responsibilities of the saints is the only other one that I put on the list. As the research started for this 75 day period, I found no other treatment of this event. The only place I found this event on a list was in Mark Hitchcock's book, *The End*. Hitchcock says the additional 45 days may be necessary for the setting up of the governmental machinery for carrying on the rule of Christ. [119] It is believed that what we do here on earth is training for what we will do in the millennium. This just might be what God intends. Look at Ephesians, Chapter 4, verse 11: *"And he gave some, apostles; and some, prophets; and some, evangelists; and some, pastors and teachers."* [120] In verse one of the chapter, Paul says *"I beseech you that ye walk worthy of the vocation wherewith ye are called."* [121] Israel will be much larger than it is today. It will stretch from the Mediterranean Sea on the west to the Euphrates River on the east (Genesis 15:18) where the Lord made a covenant with Abram concerning the land area. Actually, when Jesus Christ gets his millennial kingdom set up, all the nations of the earth will be subject to his rule. Jesus Christ will rule from Jerusalem. The saints will rule and reign with him. Jesus Christ will need many saints to help in governing all the nations of the earth. It seems to me that many appointments will have to be made in the administration of the millennial kingdom. Jesus Christ has taken care of this need with the help of the saints. Consider the following:

Revelation 3:21	2 Timothy 2:12
Revelation 5:10	Daniel 7:21-22
Revelation 20:4	Isaiah 32:1
Luke 22:30	Revelation 2:26-28

This list is not exhaustive.

Earlier, I made reference to the belief that what we do here on earth is training for what we will do in the millennium. I agree with Mark Hitchcock. He says, "What an exciting prospect! We will rule the nations with Christ for a thousand years on earth. We will even judge the angels." He writes: [122]

> *"During this present age, God is testing believers to determine their future position of authority and responsibility in the millennial kingdom. Believers will be given rulership in the kingdom over men and angels based on what we did with the treasures and talents God entrusted us with here on earth (Luke 19:11-26).*
>
> *Some will be governors over ten cities; some will rule over five cities. All believers will reign, but the extent and responsibility of that reign is being determined right now in your life and mine. As it has been said, "this is training time for reigning time."* [123]

What an interesting statement! God is preparing us for leadership in his apprenticeship program. "Christ is not simply preparing a place for us; he is preparing us for that place." [124] The saints will rule the earth forever if we believe Daniel 7. And we must believe Daniel. We really don't have a choice. [125]

> *"14 And there was given him dominion, and glory, and a kingdom, that all people, nations, and languages should serve him: his dominion is an everlasting dominion, which shall not*

pass away, and his kingdom that shall not be destroyed."....18 But the saints of the most high shall take the kingdom, and possess the kingdom forever, even forever and ever.... 22 Until the ancient of days came and judgment was given to the saints of the most high; and the time came that the saints possessed the kingdom."

These and other verses from the book of Daniel and many other verses (Revelation 22:5, Revelation 2:26). In verse 22, Daniel uses the term "ancient of days" to refer to God. We see in these verses that the saints will take the kingdom and possess it and rule in it. Hallelujah!

God will raise David from the dead and he will serve as a regent of Christ. Here I want to establish the truth of the ruling and reigning of the saints in the millennial kingdom. There is definitely a hierarchy of authority in the millennial kingdom. We will discuss that when we get to that topic.

F. The Demolition of the Temple

This has to be part of the cleaning of the land of Israel. The demolition has to be a huge job which will include the removing of all things associated with the antichrist. All things that would bring back visions of that time will have to be removed. A cleansing of all the country of Israel, if you will. Then pure and true worship can occur. This will all take time and so 75 days will be needed.

G. The Building of the Millennial Temple

This will be a huge project. At least the beginning of that process will be necessary. There will be a large labor force coming from the "Judgment of Nations." All those who will be judged worthy to enter the millennial kingdom will provide a good number for the building of that important temple.

Jesus Christ will be ruler of the entire world. He will rule and reign from this millennial temple in Jerusalem. He will institute a theocratic form of government. Everybody on earth will be expected to live according to the precepts of this form of government. It should not be difficult for those who have entered the millennial kingdom to live as defined by this form of government. For those who get out of line, Jesus Christ will rule with a rod of iron. He will put those who desire to misbehave back in their place. There will be relative peace throughout the earth. There may be a few who wish to get out of line. But their misbehavior will not last long. There will be no wars. The bible will be the constitution of the theocracy. I believe there will be a continuous process of making sure that everybody learns the constitution. This process will be in the form of teaching. Many saints in the millennial kingdom will be teachers. No doubt these teachers will come from those whose vocation was teaching while here on earth before they entered the millennial kingdom. As it has already been said, our vocation here on earth is a training ground for much of what will be needed in the millennial kingdom. If you are a teacher in the millennial kingdom, it will be a wonderful and blessed way of serving the Lord Jesus. I am sure he will be the Superintendent of Education and he will make teaching tremendously enjoyable and those who teach will be blessed. King David will be the regent under Jesus Christ. Saints will serve under King David. Ephesians 4:1 states, *"I therefore, the prisoner of the Lord, beseech you that ye walk worthy of the vocation wherewith ye are called."* [126] It would be good to read the rest of Ephesians, Chapter 4.

Much has already been said about the ruling and reigning of the saints and it has already been mentioned there will be a hierarchy of authority.

H. Hierarchy of Authority

Much has been spoken about Jesus Christ coming back to this earth and establishing his kingdom. The literal interpretation of this is that he will rule and reign over the earth for 1,000 years. He will rule and reign from his earthly throne in Jerusalem. Jerusalem will be the capital city of Israel. It will also be the capital city of the earth. Jerusalem is the center of the earth. This is a premillennialist view where the church is raptured before the seven year tribulation and "seven years later return with Jesus Christ to this earth to set up his millennial kingdom where he will rule and reign for 1,000 years." I am a premillennialist. Premillennialism is the most popular view in understanding end-time prophecy. Let me, as Mark Hitchcock has done in his recent book, *The End*, list several modern premillennialist: Donald Grey Barnhouse, Charles C. Ryeie, John Walvoord, J. Dwight Penticost, James Montgomery Boice, J. Vernon McGee, Hal Lindsey, Tim LaHaye, John MacArthur, Adrian Rogers, David Jeremiah, Thomas Ice, Chuck Smith, and Chuck Swindol. In my judgment, these are our truly premillennial scholars. There are others. They do not agree on every point but their writings is where you start if you are a premillennialist.

There will be a hierarchy of authority in the millennial kingdom. When this theocracy is completely set up, it will bring peace to the entire earth. Arnold Fruchtenbaum gives this chain of command in his book, *The Footsteps of the Messiah*, page 401. "The chain of command in the Jewish branch of government is from messianic king, to David, to the twelve apostles, to the princes, to the judges and counselors, over all Israel, which will be serving as the head of the Gentiles." [127] "The rod of iron that will characterize the rule of the government in the kingdom will be implemented through various spheres and positions of authority." [128] Jesus Christ will not have the various types of crimes that we have here on this earth. Drug behavior will just not exist. Fraud and deception will not exist. All who enter the millennial kingdom will be saved believers. Even the sheep who come out of the Judgment of Nations will be saved. Then their children will have to accept Jesus Christ just like all the rest of us did. For those who do not, they may learn what ruling with the rod of iron means. We need to go through this hierarchy of authority so we will know clearly the rulership of the kingdom:

1. The messianic kingdom will be an absolute monarchy. A monarchy will have a definite chain of command as well as a definite line of authority. Sounds like a dictator, right? The difference being that this is a theocracy. Here, Jesus Christ is the monarch. He is the messiah. The lines of authority will be split into two lines of authority. There will be a Jewish branch of government and a Gentile branch of government. Each branch of government will have its own chain of command. So that we will know the branches of government in this monarchy form of government, see illustration.

    A. There will be many nations upon the earth. Jesus Christ will be in control of the entire earth. In Isaiah 9:6, we see that *"the government shall be upon his shoulders."* [129] There will be no end to the rule of Jesus the Messiah. In Isaiah 16:5, it says the one sitting on the throne of David *"shall be sitting thereon in truth."* [130] Sometimes when I am teaching or speaking, I hold the bible in my hand and remind the people that this that I hold in my hand is the "book of truth." The throne of the messiah will be in Jerusalem but he will rule the entire world. The saints will be ruling and reigning with Jesus Christ over the nations of the earth. Jesus Christ, the messiah, is going to rule this earth along with the saints. He is going to be looked upon as the only true God by all on earth. In Luke 1:33, the scripture says *"...and he shall reign over the house of Jacob (Israel) forever; and of his kingdom there shall be no end."* [131] What Jesus Christ is setting up when he sets up the millennial kingdom will last forever. The angel made this announcement to everyone in his word. Continue to look at the "role of angels" in God's work. Here it was the angel, Gabriel.

Jesus Christ is going to rule with a "rod of iron." Remember when the Judgment of Nations takes place, the sheep were allowed to go into the millennial kingdom. They are there to repopulate the earth. They are there in their natural bodies. When they have children, those children will have to accept Jesus as their savior just like all the saints did. For those who do not conform to the principles of God's word, they will be controlled with a "rod of iron." Psalm 2:9 says *"Thou shalt break them with a rod of iron; thou shalt dash them to pieces like a potter's vessel."* [132] There will be no wars anywhere in the world. There will be no kingdom rising against another kingdom. There will be no nation rising against another nation. Anyone who gets out of line causing conflict and consternation among the people will be put back in their place by that "rod of iron." Can you imagine living in a world where there is that kind of peace? There will be relative peace because the saints will be scattered across this earth ruling and reigning with King Jesus who is in Jerusalem with King David (who is really a prince in the rank order of things).

B. Jesus Christ, the Messiah, will be the head of this monarchy that will exist throughout the world. King

David will wear the titles of both king and prince. Fruchtenbaum says it best when he says "King David will rule over Israel. So thus, he is king. But he will be prince because he will be under the authority of the messiah." Both Gentile nations and Israel will have kings. But kings in the Gentile nations will have their natural bodies. King David will have his resurrected body. Jeremiah 30:9 clarifies this. It states, but they shall serve Jehovah their God, and David their king, whom I will raise up unto them. And in Ezekiel 34:23-24 it states:[133]

"And I will set up one shepherd over them, and he shall feed them, even my servant David; he shall feed them, and he shall be their shepherd. And I, Jehovah, will be their god, and my servant David, prince among them; I Jehovah, have spoken it."

In this verse, we see that King David is under the messiah which makes him a prince, but over Israel which makes him a king. So Israel will have both Jehovah their God and David their king. David will be both king and prince. Prince to the messiah and king to the people of Israel.

C. Next in the chain of command in the Jewish branch of government is the twelve apostles. Jesus promised the twelve apostles that they would have authority over the twelve tribes (Matthew 19:28). They will sit on a throne and judge the twelve tribes (Luke 22:28-30). Each apostle will have their own throne and that will be their jurisdiction (see illustration).

According to the illustration, the next position is princes. In Isaiah 32:1, it states: *"Behold a king shall reign in righteousness, and princes shall rule in justice."* [134] In Ezekiel 45:8 it mentions princes who are rulers and have authority in the chain of command. These will have positions of authority in the millennium. Zerubbabel may be a good example of a prince in the Jewish branch of government (Haggai 2:20-23).

D. The last groups of the chain of command in the Jewish branch of government are the judges and counselors. These are mentioned in Isaiah 1:26. These groups will have authority in dispensing of justice in the city of Jerusalem.

So the chain of command in this branch of government is from the messiah, to David, to the twelve apostles, to the princes, to the judges, and counselors.

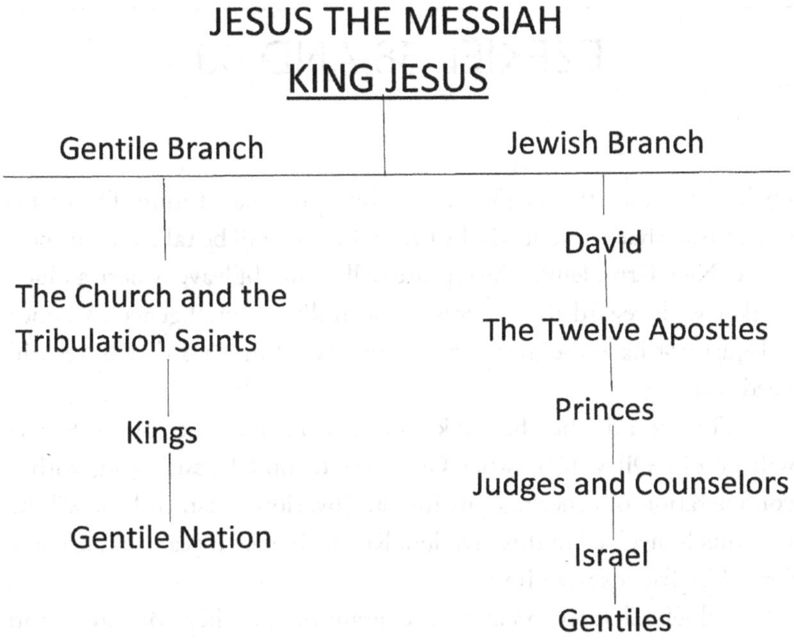

JESUS THE MESSIAH
KING JESUS

Gentile Branch	Jewish Branch

David

The Church and the
Tribulation Saints

The Twelve Apostles

Princes

Kings

Judges and Counselors

Gentile Nation

Israel

Gentiles

Illustration 1:
Dr. Arnold Fruchtenbaum, The Footsteps of the Messiah, Ariel
Ministries, 2003, p. 387.

Chapter 7

EZEKIEL 38 AND 39

I believe there are two major events in our immediate future. The first is the rapture that I described (the time when we will be taken to our new home, New Jerusalem). The rapture will no doubt leave America much weaker with regard to manpower and military intelligence. America will just not have the means to support Israel in ways that Israel will need help.

Without a doubt, the hook God will put into the jaws of Russia will be oil. Oil will be what God uses to pull Russia along with a confederation of other nations into an invasion of Israel. Iran will be very much involved in this invasion. Russia, in recent years, has become very close friends with Iran.

Ezekiel, Chapters 38 and 39, contain the prophecy of a great and massive invasion of Israel that will take place during the end times by a large confederation of nations. This large confederation will be led by Russia and will include Iran, Ethiopia, Libya, Turkey, Germany, and many others. Let us look first at those nations that make up this invading confederation.

Ezekiel 38:1-6 gives a specific list of those nations and indicates there will be others as well. Verse two states *Son of man, set thy face against Gog, the land of Magog, the chief prince of Mesheck and Tubal, and prophecy against him.* Gog is a word for ruler. Gog was "chief prince" of the land Magog. Chief is the Hebrew word "Rosh." Rosh is an ancient name for Russia. Magog is the land of Gog and is made up of three parts: Rosh, Mesheck, and Tubal. So this invasion will be led by a prince whose name is Gog. He is also in control of Mesheck (Moscow) and Tubal (Tobolsk). Tobolsk is the modern Siberian oil city located on the Tubal River. [135] Gog is a prince from a country due north of Israel. If you draw a straight line from Jerusalem due north, you will go through Moscow. In Ezekiel, Chapter 38, verse 15, it is stated this invasion will be led by the ruler of the land of Magog located in the remote parts of the north. This has to be Russia.

Persia is a nation that will be federated with Russia in this war. Persia is modern day Iran. Persia had its name changed to Iran in 1935. Other nations that make up this invading army include Ethiopia (modern nation of Sudan), Libya, Gomer (some believe Gomer to be modern day Germany, others believe Gomer to be Syria, and yet others believe Gomer to be Turkey), and other nations from Central Asia will also be included in this invasion. Other nations will also include some of the nations from the former Soviet Union.

The Psalm 83 war will be a separate war. The Psalm 83 war could very likely be fought before the start of the seven years tribulation. It will include a confederation of nations that surround the border of Israel. These are Muslim nations. Israel will fight this war and win a tremendous victory. Psalm 83 states:[136]

2 "For lo, thine enemies make a tumult: and they that hate thee have lifted up the head. 3 They have taken crafty counsel against thy people, and consulted against thy hidden ones. 4 They have said, come, and let us cut them off from being a nation; that the name of Israel may be no more in remembrance. 5 For they have consulted together with one consent: they are confederate against thee."

The Psalm 83 war will defeat the Muslim nations and wipe out terrorism in the world.

Russia is the nation that is located in the extreme or uttermost part north of Israel. Russia will lead this confederation and will invade Israel from the north. The invasion will come to the "mountains of Israel" located in the northern part of the country (verse 8). Ezekiel, Chapter

38, verse 9, states *Thou shall ascend and come like a storm, thou shall be like a cloud to cover the land, thou, and all thy land, and many people with thee.* Ezekiel had to use the words of his day to describe this invasion. In verse 9 "a cloud to cover the land" sounds like a huge wave of paratroopers maybe numbering into the thousands or it could be a large number of helicopters. "Like a storm" sounds like something massive, loud, or noisy. A storm with its lightning and thunder and rain can be noisy and sometimes frightening. Israel is a small country and it is easy to imagine how massive this can be when you think of all the military forces of the invading nations. There will be a large number of land or foot soldiers. There will be tanks from these nations rumbling across the mountains of northern Israel. There will also be airplanes dropping their bombs, perhaps nuclear. This war will be a very short war maybe no longer than a few days, perhaps even less. God will intervene and destroy the enemy of Israel. Israel will not fight this war and Israel will never be wiped off the map (John 10:28-29).

We must remember that God is in control. The prophet Isaiah has said of Israel "no weapon that is formed against you shall prosper." Obviously, the invading armies were not familiar with this verse. Because they were not, Gog and Magog and the other Arab radical Islamic Muslims invading alliances will be destroyed by God upon the mountains of northern Israel. This destruction will be so complete that less than 17 percent of these armies will survive. The invading nations never read Amos 9:15 where it is stated *"And I will plant them upon their land, and they shall no more be pulled up out of their land which I have given them, saith the Lord thy God."* This verse has to be true and since it is true, Israel has to still be in existence at the end of the seven years tribulation.

How will God destroy these godless invaders? He will use the weapons that he has always used: earthquakes (Ezekiel 38:19-20), infighting (Ezekiel 38:21), disease (Ezekiel 38:22), torrential rain, hailstones, fire, and burning sulphur (Ezekiel 38:22). An earthquake will be felt by all of God's creatures on earth, the fish of the sea, the birds of the air, the beast of the field, and every creature that moves along the ground, and all the people on the face of the earth will tremble at his presence. The mountains will be overturned, the cliffs will crumble, and every wall will fall to the ground (Ezekiel 38:19-20). Infighting will take place among the troops of the various nations. *"Every man's sword will be against his brother"* (Ezekiel 38:21). The chaos of the earthquake will cause the armies to turn against each other. These invaders will experience a plague and massive bloodshed. God has often used a plague to attack the enemies of Israel (Isaiah 37:36). Ezekiel 38:22 says .....*"I will rain upon him, and upon his lands, and upon the many people that are with him, an overflowing rain, and great hailstones, fire, and brimstone."* Major flooding would certainly hinder warfare. It would cause confusion in communication. It would be easy to see with all this judgment taking place how those fighting would become confused and start fighting among themselves. Hailstones that weigh 100 pounds and burning sulphur should remind them of how God destroyed Sodom and Gomorrah. In verse 23, God said: *"And so I will show my greatness and my holiness, and I will make myself known in the sight of many nations. Then they will know that I am the Lord."* [137]

My friend, evangelist Gary Fisher, makes a few trips to Israel every year. On a trip in 2005, the tour guide took them up to a high point on the Golan Heights. They reached an overlook so that they could see from one high top to another. What they saw were large eagles with wing spans of about seven feet. Eagles have been at this site for years but for some unexplained reason in the last few years they have been multiplying at a rapid rate. In the last few years other large birds including the Honey Buzzard, the Lesser Spotted Eagle, the Steppe Eagle, the Steppe Buzzard, and the Black Kite have been seen. God says in Ezekiel 39:4 *"I will give thee unto the ravenous birds of every sort, and to the beast of the field to be devoured."*[138] It is evident that God is getting ready for an event in Israel.

It is interesting to note that not all nations bordering Israel are listed in Ezekiel 38:5-6. This may be because these countries have fought a Psalm 83 war and Israel has won this war and expanded its (Israel) borders. The countries that border Israel but are not listed include: Lebanon, Syria, Jordon, Saudi Arabia, and maybe Egypt. I say maybe Egypt because this country is separated from Israel only by the Sinai Peninsula. All of these nations are Muslim nations. You can be sure they will be part of this invasion. All of these nations would love to see Israel out of the way. Jordan and Egypt have peace treaties with Israel today. Some of these nations have been in war with Israel before. They know Israel has much better military capabilities than they do. The nations that do not border Israel but are included in Ezekiel 38:5-6 include Germany and Turkey. The countries that have commendable militaries include Russia, Iran, Germany, and Turkey. Russia has the atomic bomb. One would think that such a massive military confederation as this could handle a small country as Israel. And they probably could but remember Israel will win this war without fighting. When this invading force comes across the mountains of Northern Israel it is going to make God angry. The first thing God is going to do is send a great earthquake that will shake the whole earth. Everyone will know that He is the Lord. From here, God will use the forces he always uses when he has to go against a nation in war (note his forces discussed previously). This war is going to be a very short war. Syria will lob a missile into Israel. Israel will respond by lobbing a bomb over into the center of downtown Damascus fulfilling Isaiah 17:1. *"Damascus is taken away from being a city and it shall be a ruinous heap."* [139]

There are several interesting reasons why Russia would like to help "wipe Israel off the map" and control the Middle East. There are several major reasons why Russia has an interest in dominating Israel including the desire to cash in on the wealth of Israel (Ezekiel 38:11-12). Israel is a much more wealthy country than most people think. Their agriculture came from a wondering Bedovin communal people who worked the swamps and deserts of Syria, Palestine, and other North African countries trying to find an existence to today where Israel is a major producer and exporter of agricultural produce. Israel, from those Bedovin communal groups, has learned how to improve the soil by planting trees and irrigation. They have become an exporter of citrus fruits, flowers, and vegetables. Israel has truly made the desert blossom and bloom just as the scriptures predicted. Israel is also an exporter of diamonds from their diamond industry. They produce and export high tech items including computers and telecom, software, and hardware. They produce medical equipment and drugs. They are a producer of precision tools and military equipment. There is a massive underground flow of oil and gas into Israel from the Mediterranean Sea. When they get oil and gas fields in Israel, it will surely wet the appetite of Russia. Russia has oil but it is so very difficult and expensive to get to it. If Russia could control Israel and the Middle East, they could have the oil they need to become the major military power of the world which is what they desire most. To do so, they need better shipping lanes than they have at the present time. Having better shipping lanes would provide their country with world markets that hinder their growth at the present time. Accessing world trading centers is now expensive and difficult. So Russia needs a warm water seaport. Russia needs a western seaport on the Mediterranean Sea. That would open world trade to Russia that would be the main ingredient for her becoming what she needs. When this flow of oil and gas into Israel is opened up, Russia will become a strong and wealthy nation. Today, she puts most of her GNP into the military. Russia does a poor job of feeding her people. Although all countries have their poor, Israel is doing a better job with her agriculture and food products. To get to the shipping ports that Russia needs, her ships must take a route that is difficult to navigate. Through the Black Sea, through the narrow lane of Bosporus, through the Seas of Marmara and the Aegean is a difficult route to have to travel to get to the Mediterranean Sea. To control Israel and the Middle East would make Russia a very powerful influence in that part of the world. Iraq, with her oil, is very attractive to Russia. The mineral deposits in the Dead Sea are great. The Dead Sea is the most mineral rich body of water in the world. It has a high concentration of minerals such as sodium, potassium, calcium, bromine, and magnesium. It also has a high concentration of sulphur. There are 21 minerals in the Dead Sea. Twelve of these are not found in any other body of water. There are several different rock types such as granite, other igneous rocks, acidic silicates, gravel, clay, sandstone, rock salt, and alluvial deposits. It is estimated that there are two billion tons of potassium chloride,

22 billion tons of magnesium chloride, and 12 billion tons of sodium chloride in the Dead Sea. [140]

If the rapture takes place before the Ezekiel 38 war, it will leave America a much weaker nation. There are more Christians in America than in Russia or any other nation. The rapture will take many Christians away from the American military, the economy, the government at all levels, and the education system.

As stated previously, Russia is a poor country and not doing a very good job of feeding its people. This is because agriculture in Russia is a failure. All these minerals could do wonders for their agriculture and the production of food products. When Russia sees this kind of weakness in America, too weak to strike back if she invades Israel, she and her Muslim allies will invade Israel. This will be the Ezekiel 38 and 39 war. I suggest we keep our eyes on the Syria-Israel relationship. This could ignite the Ezekiel 38 war.

God says that he will bring Russia into this battle. Ezekiel 38:4 states: *"And I will turn thee back, and put hooks into thy jaws, and I will bring thee forth, and all thine army, horses, and horsemen, all of them clothed with all sorts of armor, even a great company with bucklers and shields, all of them handling swords."* [141]

The reasons for this are because Russia has always been anti-semitic. A Russian dictator will lead an Arab Islamic confederation of nations to crush Israel. God will judge Russia in the land of Israel and Russia and their confederation will be destroyed.

Some of the events after the destruction of Russia and her allies include:

1. The great feast for the birds of the air and the beasts of the field eating the dead. A more thorough account of this feast is given in Ezekiel, Chapter 39:17-22. [142]

   17 "And thou son of man, thus saith the Lord God; speak unto every feathered fowl, and to very beast of the field, assemble yourselves, and come; gather yourselves on every side to my sacrifice that I do sacrifice for you, even a great sacrifice upon the mountains of

Israel, that ye may eat flesh, and drink blood. 18 Ye shall eat the flesh of the mighty, and drink the blood of the princes of the earth, of rams, of lambs, and of goats, of bullocks, all of them fattings of Bashan. 19 And ye shall eat fat till ye be full, and drink blood till ye be drunken, of my sacrifice which I have sacrificed for you. 20 Thus ye shall be filled at my table with horses, and chariots, with mighty men, and with all men of war, saith the Lord God. 21 And I will set my glory among the heathen, and all the heathen shall see my judgment that I have executed, and my hand that I have executed, and my hand that I have laid upon them. 22 So the house of Israel shall know that I am the Lord their God from that day and forward."

2. Although the time of this war will be short, probably one to three days, Jesus Christ who will fight this war will slaughter millions in this mass invasion of this confederation. Dead bodies will be lying on the ground for at least the northern half of Israel. There will be so many dead bodies that it will take Israel seven years to bury the dead. God is going to give Gog a place in Israel to bury his multitude. This place in Israel is going to be called The Valley of Hamon-gog. This cleansing of the land of Israel will provide continual employment for a number of men. Even after the seven years of burying the dead, those who pass through the land of Israel and find men's bones will set up a sign by it, till the buriers have buried them in the Valley of Hamon-gog. The burying of the dead will be of such magnitude that a city will be raised to meet the needs of those who are employed to bury the dead. The name of the city shall be called Hamonah (Ezekiel 38:10-16). It is worth taking note that Russia who has had a history of anti-Semitism will be judged and destroyed and buried in the country they hated so much. Makes you think of the verse in Genesis 12:3 that says *"And I will bless them that bless thee, and curse him that curseth thee: and in thee shall all families of the earth be blessed."* [143]

The Jews have been returning to their homeland for some time now. Since May 14, 1948, the Jews have a homeland that they can call "their" homeland. When Israel became a sovereign nation in 1948, there were about 30,000 Jews in Israel. Today, 64 years later, there are about 8,000,000 Jews. A lot of these Jews came from Russia to their homeland. Others came from many other nations. There are about as many Jews in America as there are in Israel. A logical question would be why have large numbers of Jews not left America to go to Israel. The answer to this question is because the Jews have been treated fairly well in America. Although, there is some anti-Semitism in America, it has never been a major problem. America was the first to recognize Israel as a sovereign nation. America has been a better friend to Israel than any other nation.

No one knows when the Ezekiel 38 war will take place. If you look at what is going on in the Middle East today, you would have to conclude that it will be soon. I also believe the rapture will take place before the Ezekiel war. If this is true, we can see how very close we are to the rapture. I believe there is logical scriptural support for this. All of this will bring the anti-christ on the scene. The rapture will leave America a weak nation. Israel has to be tired of war and other nations threatening to wipe her off the map and keep her from being a nation. So she may turn to the anti-christ who will promise her safety and security. No other nation will ever wipe Israel off the map. God gave Israel to the Jews and she will become even larger than she is today (see map). I'm sure Russia has never read Amos 9:14-15 where it says: [144]

> *14 "And I will bring again the captivity of my people of Israel, and they shall build the waste cities, and inhabit them; and they shall plant vineyards, and drink the wine thereof; they shall also make gardens, and eat the fruit of them. 15 And I will plant them upon their land, and they shall no more be*

pulled up out of their land which I have given them, saith the Lord the God."

The bible is the only book of truth on the face of the earth. When God makes a promise, he keeps it. God cannot lie. I like verse 15. In this verse is strong scriptural support for what I mentioned earlier. No nation is ever going to destroy Israel or wipe her off the map.

    A. Upon "their" land
    B. No more be pulled up
    C. Their land
    D. Which I have given them

Israel is God's country. My savior is a Jew. Someday soon Jesus Christ, God's son, is going to rule and reign from Jerusalem. Jerusalem is the capital city of Israel. The capital city of earth. Israel is the center of earth. Israel as a nation will be the standard barrier of all other nations on earth. In studying prophecy, I always try to find my place in all of this. I will have a place because God promised I would rule and reign with Jesus Christ. Have you ever thought about the relationship you will have with Jesus Christ for all the rest of eternity? We should pray for the peace of Jerusalem (Psalm 122:6) and for the nation of Israel (Genesis 12:3). Israel is God's country and it is going to stay God's country. Hallelujah!

3.   Terrorism has become a major problem in the world. Terrorism centers around the hatred of those that follow a radical interpretation of Muslim religion for western nations. We hear this almost every day in the news that they will wipe Israel off the map and America is next. I believe the problem of terrorism will be solved with the Psalm 83 war. If you look at Ezekiel 38:6, it ends with *"....and many people with thee."* Israel is totally and completely surrounded by Muslim

nations. Those radical Muslims would love to see Israel out of the Middle East. If this could happen, it would get American influence out of the Middle East. Lebanon, Syria, Jordan, Saudi Arabia, and Egypt border Israel. Just due east of these nations are Iraq and Iran. Iran is listed in verse 5. To the south are United Arab eremites, Omar, and Yemen, all Muslim nations. To the west are Sudan, Egypt, Libya, Tunisia, and Algeria. All of these are Muslim nations. Sudan (Ethiopia) and Libya are listed in verse 5. So we know these nations will be involved in this mass invasion. Millions of these radical Muslims will be killed in this invasion on the mountains of northern Israel. Eighty-three percent of this invasion will be killed. The remaining force of the Russian army will be pushed back into Siberia.

4. It will take Israel seven years to burn and destroy the weapons of the invading confederation. This gives us some idea about the magnitude of weapons of this invading force. Ezekiel 38:9-10 gives us more insight into the military hardware that will be left scattered on the ground throughout northern Israel. Not only millions of dead bodies will be all over the grounds of northern Israel but there will be a mess of military hardware that will have to be cleaned up. [145]

> 9 *"And they that dwell in the cities of Israel shall go forth, and shall set on fire and burn the weapons, both the shields and the bucklers, the bows and the arrows, and the hand staves, and the spears, and they burn them with fire seven years: 10 So that they shall take no wood out of the fields, neither cut down any out of the forests; for they shall burn the weapons with fire: and they shall spoil those that spoiled them, and rob those that robbed them, saith the Lord God."*

These two verses indicate the magnitude of the military hardware used by Russia in this war. Russia is serious about this war and this massive invasion. If the rapture has taken place, it has left America weak because millions of Christians have been taken in the rapture, thus leaving insufficient military intelligence to respond to an invasion of this magnitude. If this war does not happen soon, Iran will have a nuclear bomb. Russia already has many nuclear bombs. Would they use them? Iran would. I'm not sure God would allow Iran to drop a nuclear bomb on his country. One nuclear bomb dropped on Israel would just about destroy that nation. God has already promised that once the Jews are back in their homeland, they shall never again be rooted up and displaced. With America too weak to respond, Russia can just see herself setting on the coast of the Mediterranean in total and complete control of Israel and the rest of the Middle East. With all the wealth in Israel spoken of above and all the wealth of the rest of the oil rich Middle East, Russia could truly dominate the world. Would Russia drop a nuclear bomb on Israel? I do not believe she would because I do not believe Russia believes she would need to. Russia probably has a higher superior military force than Israel. With all the other countries, Russia would feel there would be no need to drop a nuclear bomb. Ezekiel 38 indicates Russia would believe she has a mighty army with her. Ezekiel 39:9, 15, & 16 states: [146]

> 9 *"Thou shalt ascend and come like a storm, thou shall be like a cloud to cover the land, thou, and all thy bands, and many people with thee. 15....and a mighty army. 16....as a cloud to cover the land."*

So Russia has to believe she can defeat Israel. But what Russia does not know is Israel is not going to fight this war. God is going to fight this war and Russia is no match for God. God is going to draw Russia to the Jewish homeland, into the place where Russia has persecuted the Jews throughout all history.

God is going to end that persecution in the homeland of the Jews.

It is difficult to imagine that the amount of military hardware scattered across the northern half of Israel will take seven years to burn. This is one reason I believe the Ezekiel 38 war will take place before the seven years tribulation begins. When Jesus Christ returns to this earth to set up his millennial kingdom, he does not have time to clean up a mess left behind. I do not find in the scripture where any time will be given by Christ to cleaning up weapons of war when he returns to earth. He has so many more important things he will be busy doing. He does not need used weapons of war to be in his way.

There will be so many used weapons from the Ezekiel 38 war that it will take seven years to burn all of it. There will be no need for Israel to "take wood out of the field" or "cut down any of the forests" (Ezekiel 39:10).

Chapter 8

VIEW OF THE FUTURE

Almost all writers of prophecy have some view about how all of this is going to come together. I believe if you look at what is taking place in the Middle East at the present time, you have to believe the pieces of the puzzle are coming together. What is about to happen in the world today? This is a good and fair question to ask. If you ask me to write down a scenario of what I see happening, the following is what I would predict. Some writers would agree with me for the most part; others would not. All writers are trying to understand God's word and we all better stay close to the scripture.

When you are trying to determine the place, when the rapture will occur, and when the events in Ezekiel 38 will happen, we need to remember the rapture will take place before the tribulation period begins. We do not know when before the seven years tribulation the rapture will take place but scripture tells us it will. The rapture is a signless event. Nothing else has to happen before the rapture takes place. It is an imminent event. It can take place at any time. For our post-tribulation friends, the rapture is not an imminent event. For them, the rapture will take place at the end of the seven years tribulation period. For the pre-tribulation believers, the seven years tribulation is not imminent. It will begin with the signing of the peace covenant by the antichrist and Israel. When that signing takes place, the church will have already been raptured to heaven. God has made several promises indicating the church will not have to go through the wrath of the tribulation. The following is a partial list of those promises:

1. Revelation 3:10

    "Because thou has kept the word of my patience, I also will keep thee from the hour of temptation, which shall come upon all the world, to try them that dwell upon the earth." [147] Earlier, I mentioned the best interpretation of scripture is a literal interpretation. We do not need to trust the meaning of scripture to fit the mold of who we are. Rather, we need to fit ourselves to the scripture. That phase, *"will keep thee from the hour of temptation"* refers to the time of tribulation. *"Which shall come upon all the world"* supports that phrase that it is the tribulation. In this verse God is promising the church that because you have kept my word, then I will keep you from the hour of temptation or the hour of tribulation.

2. 1 Thessalonians 1:10

    "And to wait for this son from heaven, whom he raised from the dead, even Jesus, which delivered us from the wrath to come." [148] To not be "waiting for his son from heaven" would rob us of Titus 2:13. Jesus is going to deliver us from the wrath to come. The "wrath to come" starts with the tribulation. The rapture happens before the tribulation begins.

3. 1 Thessalonians 5:9

    "For God hath not appointed us to wrath, but to obtain salvation by our Lord Jesus Christ." [149] Wrath starts with the tribulation. The first part of this verse tells us that *"God hath not appointed us to wrath."* But he has appointed us to obtain salvation by Jesus Christ. What is salvation? Salvation is the saving of those who will believe on the Lord Jesus Christ. What are we saved from? We are saved from death brought on by the anti-christ

and the tribulation. We are not looking for the tribulation. We are looking for that blessed hope (Titus 2:13).

4. Romans 5:9

    "Which more then, being now justified by his blood, we shall be saved from wrath through him." [150] I have stated the wrath of God begins with the seven years tribulation. This verse tells us the church will be saved from wrath through him.

5. Luke 21:36

    "Watch ye therefore, and pray always, that ye may be accounted worthy to escape all these things that shall come to pass, and to stand before the son of man." [151] Look at the phrase "that ye may be accounted worthy to escape all these things that shall come to pass." This is clearly a warning to those that Jesus was teaching about his return. Jesus was promising them that they would be accounted worthy to escape the time of wrath if they would "watch" and "pray."

Each of these five verses tells us that the rapture is a pre-tribulation rapture. We still cannot determine the date when the rapture will happen. The scripture does not tell us. Only that it will happen before the tribulation. There are many other verses (Matthew 3:7, Luke 3:7, Revelation 4:1, Revelation 6:17) that tell us the rapture is a pre-trib event. John Walvoord agrees when he says "The only view that interprets prophecy literally and consistently is that of the pretribulational, premillennium position." [152]

Ezekiel 38-39: Its Place

Determining the place and time when the Ezekiel 38-39 war will take place may be more difficult than determining when the rapture will take place. Let me hasten to say the scripture does not tell us in either case when these events will take place. There are several views as to when the Ezekiel 38-39 war will take place. One popular view is that it will take place before the rapture. When you look closely at what is taking place in the world today, and particularly in the Middle East, it would be easy to agree with this position. Israel is surrounded by Muslim nations and all of them hate the Jews and would love to see them and Israel annihilated. Only Jordan and Egypt have peace treaties with Israel and both are Muslim nations. I'm sure both would fight in a large confederation of Muslim nations led by a major nation like Russia who has a strong military force thus giving that confederation a likely chance of winning the war. Remember, Jordan, Egypt, nor Russia realize they will be up against Jesus Christ in this war. This view would give Israel time to bury the dead and burn all the war material left after the war is finished. This gives strong support for this view. I believe any view which gives Israel time to clean the country of the dead bodies and clear the land of the military hardware has a favorable position as to when this war will take place. This is a strong position because the Tim LaHaye group favors this view and I am in agreement with them.

Another strong view is that this war will take place near the midpoint of the seven years tribulation. The Jack VanImpe group holds to this view. One of the major problems with this view is that it does not give Israel the seven years needed to clear the dead bodies and the military hardware left behind after the war. I cannot find any scripture that will help in understanding that there will be a continual cleaning of the country of dead bodies and military hardware (soldiers' uniforms, weapons, trucks, carriers, tanks, helicopters, airplanes, empty shells, etc.). With this view, the cleaning would carry on for 3 ½ years after Jesus returns to stop Armageddon. This view holds that the Ezekiel 38-39 war will initiate during the last 3 ½ years of the seven years tribulation period. My feelings are that this war just does not fit at this point. Remember, the last 3 ½ years of the seven will be the worst time known to man. And this will be true with or without the Ezekiel 38-39 war. Remember, the antichrist has just declared himself to be God and everyone is required to worship him. Everyone is required to take the "mark" of the beast. The "trumpet" and vial judgments are to be poured out. This war will be a short war but it will be massive with a few million involved, no doubt. This war has to happen. There has never been a war like this in the history of Israel. John Walvoord says "There has never been a war with Israel which fulfills the prophecies of Ezekiel 38-39." [153] Approximately 5/6 or 83% of this invasion will be killed. Can you imagine the job of those assigned to burying the dead and cleaning up the military scattered across northern Israel? This war simply does not fit here. It is out of place. This war is not Armageddon. It is not the war that Gog will bring against Jesus Christ near the end of the millennium. Russia has just been embarrassed by Jesus Christ. They have been pushed so far back into Siberia that it will take them a while to recover. They will not take over the wealth of Israel and the Middle East as they so much desire.

The view I feel most comfortable with is placing the Ezekiel 38-39 war between the rapture and the beginning of the tribulation. There are several major reasons why I would place this war between the rapture and the beginning of Daniel's 70th week.

1. America has been made weak by the rapture. Our country will lose a large number, perhaps millions, of its most intelligent individuals. There are more Christians in America than in any other nation. Certainly more than in Russia. After the rapture, the United States will not be able to function as a nation at a very proficient level. Much of America's high tech military hardware will be crippled. Many of America's brightest individuals who have a vast knowledge of high tech "know how" have been raptured thus leaving America militarily weak. Russia knows this.

2. America's economy has been struggling for more than a decade and she has become a weak nation. Certainly too weak to fight a major war the size of this large confederation (Russia, Iran, Libya, Ethiopia, Germany, Turkey, and many other Muslim nations). This is a major war. Russia also knows this. America is probably too weak to fight back. It has to seem to Russia

to be a good time to invade Israel. Russia is "foaming at the mouth" because of what she thinks she can have in Israel and the Middle East. It is very doubtful that the American economy will ever recover back to what it once was.

3. If the war is fought before the seven years tribulation begins, that would give Israel the seven years needed to burn the scattered and left behind military hardware. This would leave Israel a relatively clean country side when Jesus Christ returns to earth. There are so many major things Jesus Christ has to get accomplished during the 75 day period from when he stops Armageddon to when he sets up his millennial kingdom (resurrection of old testament saints, resurrection of tribulation martyrs, judgment of nations, assignment of saints). So the burning of the military hardware would not be a factor of consideration when he returns.

4. As to the question of this invasion taking place when Israel is safe and at peace is problematic. First, I do not see Israel any more at peace than they are at the present time. There are those who say the time just after the antichrist signs that peace document should provide the best time of peace. But does it? Remember the signing of the peace document initiates the seven years tribulation time. During the first 3 ½ years the seven seals of judgments are opened. The first four seals deal with the four horseman of the apocalypse. This is a time when Satan will be unleashed on this earth. This time represents war, disease, famine, starvation, corruption, and confusion. It is said that from one fourth to one half of the world's population will be killed or will die in other ways. That does not seem so peaceful to me. The last 3 ½ years of the tribulation certainly will not be a peaceful time.

5. There are two more prophecies that must find their place somewhere between now and the second coming of Christ.

Psalm 83:3-5 states *3 They have taken crafty counsel against thy people, and consulted against thy hidden ones. 4 They have said, come, and let us cut them off from being a nation; that the name of Israel may be no more in remembrance. 5 For they have consulted together with one consent: they are confederate against thee."* [154] Isaiah 17:1 says *"The burden of Damascus. Behold Damascus is taken away from being a city, and it shall be a ruinous heap."* [155] The wording in the Psalm account seems to be what we are hearing at the present time especially from Ahmadinejad in Iran. These people hate Israel and would love to see all the Jews killed. He also hates America just about as much as he hates the Jews. He has made the statement "What would the world be like without Israel and the Jews and America and Christians?" He has already told the Jews that Israel needs to be wiped off the map. The Isaiah 17:1 prophecy could be fulfilled at any moment. They have already killed over 100,000 in that civil war. One wrong move and Damascus could become that ruinous heap. The Jews are hated by the Syrians.

If this war is placed between the rapture and the beginning of the seven years tribulation, look at how close we are to the rapture. I say this because it seems the pieces of the puzzle of the Ezekiel 38 and 39 war are falling together rapidly. Unless something happens very soon, Iran will have a nuclear bomb. Would they use it? I believe they would. They hate the Jews. But I also believe they will not be effective in destroying the country of Israel. Amos 9:14-15 states:[156]

> *"14 And I will bring again the captivity of my people of Israel, and they shall build the waste cities; and inhabit them; and they shall plant vineyards, and drink the wine thereof; they shall also make gardens, and eat the fruit of them. 15 And I will plant them upon their land, and they shall no more be pulled up out of their land which I have given them, saith the Lord thy God."*

Much of what is stated in these two verses has already been fulfilled. The Jews have taken a country that was not much more than a wasteland and turned it into a thriving, prosperous county. They are already exporting agricultural produce, especially fruits. Their agricultural efforts are some of the best in the world. They have what is probably the fourth largest military in the world. Their military is an excellent force. They also have some of the best universities in the world, especially in the area of medicine. Verse 15 indicates Israel, as a country, is here to stay. They became a sovereign nation in 1948 and have fought and won six wars. They have been planted in their land. And Mr. Ahmadinejad, "they shall no more be pulled up out of their land" says their God. Israel as a country has to be in existence when Jesus Christ comes back at the end of the seven years tribulation period. So they are not going to be wiped off the map. The scripture also teaches in Luke 21:*28 "And when these things begin to come to pass, then look up, and lift up your heads; for your redemption drawth nigh."* [157] I like the way John Hagee expresses this. He says that when you see these things "you had better pack up, pray up, and look up, for we are about to go up." What kinds of things is Jesus talking about here? I believe if you made a list of all the disturbing things happening in our society and around the world this is what Jesus is talking about. Look at what is found in Luke, Chapter 21:

A. Wars and commotions

B. Nations rising against nations

C. Earthquakes in divers places

D. Famines

E. Pestilence

F. Fearful sights and great signs from heaven

G. Persecution and imprisonment for his name's sake

H. Betrayal by parents, brethren, kinsfolk, and friends causing death

   I.   Hatred of all men for his name's sake

   J.   Great distress in the land

      (1) Failing economics across the world

      (2) Fifty percent of Americans are on food stamps

      (3) One out of six live in poverty

      (4) Low compensation for work

      (5) Challenge of moral issues

- Abortion
- Homosexuality
- Same sex marriages
- Birth control
- Drugs
- Illegitimate births
- Crime
- Corruption
- Bible reading and praying in public places (school/government)
- Apostasy of our churches – Many churches have not baptized one person in several years. The churches are not growing and many are closing. Many churches have become social centers and are no longer preaching the gospel of Jesus Christ.
- Apathy - Church attendance has lost its meaning and is no longer an event looked forward to by its members.

The pieces of a one world government are coming together. If America stays on the path it is on, it will fall just as Rome did. America is on a path to becoming a second rate nation. How can America not be judged when she continues to turn her back on the principles of God's word that made her one of the greatest nations in all of history? God judged Sodom and Gomorrah because these cities were wicked and homosexuality prevailed. The government in America has become corrupt and dysfunctional. The leaders think more of themselves than they do of their country. They are extremely selfish. These are the ingredients that will cause the country to fall. They have also turned their backs on God's country, Israel. Look for an event to take place in America soon…one greater than 9/11. America may not be able to recover from this event. II Chronicles 7:14 says:[158]

> *"If my people, which are called by my name, shall humble themselves, and pray, and seek my face, and turn from their wicked ways; then will I hear from heaven, and will forgive their sin, and will heal their land."*

Chapter 9

THE MILLENNIUM

In Revelation, chapters 20 and 21 are devoted to the millennial kingdom. Beyond these chapters in the bible, there are many sources that devote space to the millennium. But they all present the same topics and issues just in different ways. So we have a general view of the millennium, Dr. Arnold Fruchtenbaum presents the most thorough and detailed account of the millennium in his book *The Footsteps of the Messiah.* [159]

The government in the millennium will surely be a theocracy. The theocratic government is God's idea of a perfect government. The rulership in this government is in one person…the Lord Jesus Christ. He will rule and reign from Jerusalem. King David will be a regent and will also rule and reign with King Jesus from Jerusalem. King David will also be a prince and in this sense will be under King Jesus the messiah. This form of government is a monarchy in the sense that absolute sovereignty is found in one great king. Jesus Christ will be that one great king. He will be the king over this whole earth. If anyone get out of line, he will put them back in place because he will rule with a rod of iron. When the millennial kingdom starts, there will be four groups of people. The raptured saints, the Old Testament saints, the tribulation martyrs, and the sheep who came out of the "Judgement of Nations" (the sheep-goats judgement).

The entire earth will experience relative peace. All of the above groups will be saved believers. The role of the sheep will be to repopulate the earth. As time moves forward, the children born of this group will have to accept Jesus Christ as their savior just like all others did. All members of the earth will be expected to live by the precepts of the word of God…the bible. The bible is the constitution of this monarchy. The reason there will be relative peace is because of the manifestation of the new covenant by the population of the earth (Jeremiah 31:31-34).

> *"Behold, the days come, says Jehovah, that I will make a new covenant with the house of Israel, and with the house of Judah: not according to the covenant that I made with their fathers in the day that I took them by the hand to bring them out of the land of Egypt; which my covenant they broke, although I was a husband unto them, say Jehovah. But this is the covenant that I will make with the house of Israel after those days, says Jehovah: I will put my law in their inward parts, and in their heart will I write it; and I will be their God, and they shall be my people: and they shall teach no more every man his neighbor, and every man his brother, saying, Know Jehovah; for they shall all know me, from the least of them unto the greatest of them, says Jehovah: for I will forgive their iniquity, and their sin will I remember no more."*

So the reason there will be peace throughout the earth is because God will write "his law in the hearts of the people" and all will know proper behavior according to God's law. If anyone steps outside of God's law they will be punished. He will rule with a rod of iron. All the Jews in the millennium will know the Lord Jesus Christ as messiah. He has forgiven them of their sins and he will remember them no more.

Another reason there will be peace throughout the land is because the curse will be lifted. Peace will exist between man and man, between animal and animal, and between man and animal.[160] I have been teaching a prophecy class at our church for several years. When we get on the topic of the millennium, I "joke" with my class telling them that when we get to the millennium, I am going to get a big fuzzy bear for a buddy. He will know me and I will know him. I have told them I am going to name him "Whisle." It will be true that we will not have fear of animals and animals will not have fear of man. That carnivorous instinct among animals will be removed. Animals will not seek meat for food. They will eat straw (no doubt hay, wheat, corn) (Isaiah 11:7). This indicates to me that there will be an agricultural industry in the millennium. The scripture says straw (Isaiah 11:6-9). Where is the straw going to come from to feed all of these animals? And will it be just straw? Also the sheep (man) who go into the millennium will have their natural bodies. They will have to eat (see Isaiah 65:21-25). So there will have to be an agricultural effort to feed all the animals and man (Isaiah 65:21-25). Man will no doubt be vegetarian. There will be animals all around him. God will not approve that man kill animals for food (Isaiah 66:3). Since the curse is lifted even the soil will be rich and productive. Crops of hay, wheat, corn, and garden will not have thorns, grass, and weeds to contend with. Grapes, tomatoes, corn, peas, beans, potatoes, and fruit of all kinds will be more productive. Produce will be larger, smoother, juicier, and without being stained by insects. This industry will be so much easier to work in because the curse has been lifted. In the millennium, there will be no poor or hunger.

In the millennium, saints will be assigned all kinds of things to do. We will be busy but there will also be plenty of time for rest, fun, fellowship, and worship. In my earthly life, I have always been a singer. I believe I will be able to find my singing friends in heaven and continue to sing. I know there will be plenty of time for worship, true worship of the Lord Jesus. There will be time for fun. Remember, we will be in New Jerusalem. It will be so beautiful there are no words to describe it. Remember, Paul was caught up to the third heaven, paradise, and could not describe what he saw (see II Corinthians 12:2-4). Paul "heard unspeakable words which it is not lawful for a man to utter." I have an idea that New Jerusalem will be so beautiful that we may never get used to that kind of beauty. It will be a lot of fun fellowshipping with so many of our family, friends, and loved ones. Then there are Job, Daniel, Jeremiah, Isaiah, Abraham, Ezekiel, Melchizedek, John, Paul, Peter, Billy Graham and we will have all eternity to talk to them.

I happen to love flowers of all kinds. Particularly flowers that bloom. There are bushes that bloom such as rose and many other different kinds. My son gives his mother two bougainvillea plants each

Mother's Day. Several years ago, our family went to Hawaii for a week. We found different colors of bougainvillea growing along fence rows. They were of different colors. How beautiful! Then there are small trees like Crape Myrtles that bloom in different colors. How beautiful! The flower world during the millennium will be more beautiful than what we see on earth now because the curse has been lifted. Particularly because the soil will be more conducive to growing flowers. We will not have to fight grass, weeds, disease, and other growth that hinders the growth of flowers. Flowers in the millennium will be larger, prettier, and without blemish because we will live in a world more like what God intended in the Garden of Eden. Saints will rule and reign over this part of the millennial government. The saints who will be assigned these jobs will truly have a beautiful job. Can you imagine the smell of all those beautiful, perfect flowers?

A. Covenants

I have heard it said that there is just not much information about the millennial kingdom but once I began searching, I found more than I thought I would. For example, there are four unfulfilled covenants God made with Israel and we have just about run out of time for them to be fulfilled. Since God keeps his promises, they must be fulfilled and it seems he plans to use the 1,000 years millennium time to fulfil these covenants. A brief understanding of these covenants is too important to leave them out of this writing. A brief description of the four covenants is found in Dr. Arnold Fruchtenbaum's book, *The Footsteps of the Messiah.* [161]

1. Abrahamic Covenant

This covenant promised an eternal seed that would develop into a nation that would possess the Promised Land with "definite borders." The Jews have never possessed all of the Promised Land. So there must be a future kingdom where this promise may be fulfilled. God said to Abraham *"to you will I give it, and to your seed forever.*"(Genesis 13:15). God will fulfill this through Abraham and through his seed of Isaac and Jacob. This will happen during the 1,000 years millennial kingdom.

At this writing, they are fighting in Israel over who should possess the land of Israel. The Palestinians believe the Jews are occupying their land. The Jews believe the land of Israel was given to them by God. The Abrahamic Covenant was given to Abraham by God and the land area will be so much larger than it is today. Someday, the Jews will occupy the land that was promised to them by God.

2. The Palestinian Covenant

This is the land covenant. This requires a worldwide regathering of the Jews. The Jews have never claimed all the "land" that was promised to them. Their land will include all land from the Mediterranean Sea on the west to the Euphrates River on the East to a part of Syria on the north to part of Saudi Arabia on the south (this is part of Iraq). Israel has been a sovereign nation since 1948, and several million Jews (about 8 million) have gathered back in their homeland. Jews continue to return to Israel from all over the world. But the repossession of the Promised Land has not fully happened. It will happen during the 1,000 years millennium when Jesus sets up his earthly kingdom.

3. The Davidic Covenant

This covenant requires four eternal things: (1) an eternal house, (2) an eternal throne, (3) an eternal kingdom, (4) and one eternal person. When Jesus sets up his earthly kingdom, all four of these things will be fulfilled.

4.   The New Covenant

This speaks to the salvation of Israel. This too will be realized when Jesus Christ sets up his millennial kingdom. From these four covenants, the millennial kingdom will have its beginning. With Jesus Christ, the messiah, ruling over this kingdom. The beginning of this kingdom may not be so far away.

There are four "facets" to the final restoration of Israel. Each of these facets are attached to a specific covenant according to Dr. Arnold Fruchtenbaum. Look at the following:

A.   The first facet is the national regeneration of Israel. The basis of Israel's final regeneration is attached to the New Covenant (see Jeremiah 31:31-34). [162] This new covenant will be a total national regeneration of Israel.[163] Jewish missions and Jewish evangelism will not be needed in the messianic kingdom because every Jew will know the Lord, from the least to the greatest." [164] Jehovah will forgive all the sins of Israel to remember them no more. When the law is written in our hearts that will be the way we will know to behave. There will be no need to teach brother or neighbor. They will already know. All Jews will be believers in the kingdom. The Jews will already know him.

Some may wonder why all the attention is on Israel today. It is just a very small country....but it is God's country. From the very beginning, God chose Israel as his country. The Jews have sinned all across their history. They were in bondage in Egypt and finally pharaoh let them go. They spent 40 years in a desert wilderness without food and water but God provided. God rained down food from heaven and provided water by simply striking a rock and water gushed forth enough to satisfy the people and all the animals. They were held in captivity for 70 years in Babylon. They were freed and became scattered all over the world. Today, they are returning to that country and God is going to forgive them of their sins to remember them no more. God has "blotted out" their sins and has redeemed Israel. *"Israel shall be saved with an everlasting salvation and their shame will be put to an end."* [165] Many times in the prophecy class that I teach, the question comes up "what language will we speak?" I tell them it will be the only pure language and that is Hebrew (Zephaniah 3:9)

B. "The second facet of the final restoration of Israel is the regathering of Israel from all over the world." [166] One of the major, major things of the "end times" is the regathering of the Jews to their homeland. This facet is attached to the land covenant (Deuteronomy 29:1-30: 20).

This regathering is the first regathering and has been going on since 1948. It is in preparation for judgement. It is "in preparation for the millennial blessing." [167] It is characterized by being a worldwide regathering. This will be the final regathering for the Jews. One major advantage of this regathering of the Jews to their homeland will be a uniting of Israel and Judah. So Israel will be a nation without division. This gathering will be a total regathering of the Jews back to Israel. Jews will be rescued from their enemies. Praise God. They have been persecuted all across time. It will be tremendous that this persecution will come to an end. The regathering will be focused on the Middle East but the regathering will be worldwide. Look at Jeremiah 16:15 where it says *"and I will bring them again into their land that I gave unto their fathers."*[168] In Ezekiel 11:14-18, it says:[169]

> *"Thus saith the Lord God; although I have cast them far off among the countries, and although I have scattered them among the countries, yet will I be to them as a little sanctuary in the countries where they shall come....Thus saith the Lord God; I will even gather you from the people, and assemble*

you out of the countries where ye have been scattered, and I will give you the land of Israel."

A minor prophet that I have used so many times is Amos. This scripture says:[170]

"And I will bring back the captivity of my people Israel, and they shall build the waste cities, and inhabit them; and they shall plant vineyards, and drink the wine there of; they shall also make gardens, and eat the fruit of them. And I will plant them upon their land, and they shall no more be plucked up out of their land which I have given them, says Jehovah your God."

"The Jews will never again depart from the Lord." [171] Angels will bring the Jews back into the land. The role of angels in God's plan is so awesome. This worldwide regathering of the Jews as shown above will be fulfilled only after the second coming and the beginning of the millennium. In Matthew 24:31, we find this verse: *"And he shall send forth his angels with a great sound of a trumpet, and they shall gather together his elect from the four winds, from one end of heaven to the other."* [172]

C. The third facet of the restoration of Israel is the possession of the land. Here we look at Israel's total boundaries and its productivity. The Abrahamic Covenant provides the basis for this facet. God told Abram in Genesis 13:14-17 that he would give him *"all the land which you see, to you I will give it, and to your seed forever"....arise, walk through the land in the length of it and in the breadth of it; for unto you will I give it."* [173] In Genesis 15:12-21, the exact boundaries are given. God told Abram that unto your seed have I given this land, from the river of Egypt unto the great river, the river Euphrates. This has to be the eastern boundaries. On the west, the Mediterranean Sea is the boundary. The Abrahamic Covenant will confirm and restore this land to Israel. It will be much larger land than the small area they possess (see illustration, p.164-165). There will also be a great increase in productivity. That is happening today. Why is this increase in productivity happening? Look at the following:

(1) And I will give rain for your seed (Isaiah 30:23-26).

(2) In that day shall your cattle feed in large pastures (Isaiah 30:23-26).

(3) There shall be brooks and streams of water (Isaiah 30:23-26). Look at how both man and animals will be served.

(4) They shall build houses and inhabit them (Isaiah 65:21-24).

(5) They shall plant vineyards, and eat the fruit of them (Isaiah 65:21-24).

(6) His chosen shall long enjoy the work of their hands (Isaiah 65:21-24).

(7) Before they call, I will answer; while they are yet speaking, I will hear (Isaiah 65:21-24).

(8) The desert shall rejoice, and blossom as the rose (Isaiah 35:1-2).

(9) The desert shall blossom abundantly (Isaiah 35:1-2).

(10) The planters shall plant, and shall enjoy the fruit thereof (Jeremiah 31:1-6).

(11) To the grain, and to the new wine: and to the oil, and to the young of the flock and of the heard: and their soul shall be as a watered garden; and they shall not sorrow any more (Jeremiah 31:11-14).

(12) They shall dwell securely therein; yea, they shall build houses, and plant vineyards, and shall dwell securely (Ezekiel 28:25-26).

(13) The tree of the field shall yield its fruit, and the earth shall yield its increase (Ezekiel 35:25-31).

(14) They shall be secure in their land (Ezekiel 35:25-31).

(15) They shall know that I am Jehovah (Ezekiel 35:25-31).

(16) Neither shall the beasts of the earth devour them (Ezekiel 35:25-31).

(17) And none shall make them afraid (Ezekiel 35:25-31).

(18) There shall be no more famine in the land (Ezekiel 35:25-31).

(19) No, enemies or wild beasts, will come to destroy the crops (Ezekiel 35:25-31).

(20) The production of the land will be tremendous (Ezekiel 35:25-31).

(21) Waste places shall be builded and land that was desolate shall be tilled (Ezekiel 36:28-38).

(22) This land that was desolate is become like the Garden of Eden (Ezekiel 36:28-38).

(23) The rains will come at the proper seasons and in the proper amounts causing a tremendous amount of surplus in their storages (Ezekiel 36:28-38).

(24) The floors shall be full of wheat, the vats shall overflow with new wine and oil (Ezekiel 36:28-38).

I am absolutely overwhelmed. Israel will possess their land and the land will produce abundantly. No one will be hungry. There will be no poor. This above is on the basis of the Abrahamic covenant. The saints will be in New Jerusalem. Jesus will be there in his earthy kingdom. Hallelujah!

D. The fourth facet is the reestablishment of the Davidic Throne. This is based upon the Davidic Covenant. We can see the Davidic Covenant in two different scriptures: 2 Samuel and 1 Chronicles. It is stated in 2 Samuel 7: [174]

"I will establish his kingdom. He shall build a house for my name, and I will establish the throne of his kingdom forever. I will be his father, and he shall be my son: if he commit iniquity, I will chasten him with the rod of man....but my

loving kindness shall not depart from him, as I took it from Saul, whom I put away before you. And your house and your kingdom shall be made sure forever before you: your throne shall be established forever. David is the head of a dynasty."

After David dies, the throne goes to Solomon, his son. The kingdom then is established in his hand. Solomon will build the millennial temple. Solomon sins and God punishes him but does not remove his love from him. The Davidic Kingdom, the Davidic House of Dynasty, and the Davidic Throne will be eternal. In this scripture, the attention has been on Solomon. In the second scripture, 1 Chronicles 17:10-14, the attention will be on the messiah. In the first passage Solomon, one of David's sons is spoken of. In the second passage, David's son, Jesus, is named. Here God builds the millennial temple and his throne will be established forever. Here, King Jesus is stablished forever. The Davidic Covenant guarantees four eternal things: a dynasty, a kingdom, a throne, and a person. There must be a Davidic Throne for Jesus to sit on, to rule as king over Israel and King of the World. This all begins with the Second Coming. Psalm 89:29 says "His seed will I make to endure forever, and his throne as the days of heaven." [175]

Psalm 89:34-37 says:[176]

"My covenant will I not break, nor alter the thing that is gone out of my lips. Once have I sworn by my holiness: I will not lie unto David: his seed shall endure forever, and his throne as the sun before me. It shall be established forever as the moon, and as the faithful witness in the sky.

Since God does not lie, the covenant is sure to stand.

In Luke 1:32-33, we find the reestablishment of the Davidic Throne:[177]

> *"He shall be great, and shall be called the Son of the Most High: and the Lord God shall give unto him the throne of his father David: and he shall reign over the house of Jacob forever; and of his kingdom there shall be no end."*

This certainly carries over into eternity. At the end of the millennium, Jesus Christ will be recommissioned and will not lose his kingship. He shall rule over Israel and the world forever.

B. Millennial Jerusalem

When Jesus Christ returns to Israel and plants his feet on the "Mount of Olives" a very great earthquake will take place. It will shake the entire earth. Tall buildings all over the world will fall down (emphasis mine). They will crumble to the ground. That ought to tell the whole world Jesus Christ is back to earth in all his power. When he plants his feet on the "Mount of Olives," one half of that mount will be pushed to the north and one half of that mount will be pushed to the south creating a large valley that will run east and west. It will do two major things. First, it will provide a way for the Jews to escape and second it will create a major place for Israel to tremendously increase its production of agricultural products of all kinds. Remember with the start of the millennium, the curse will be lifted. The land will be much more fertile and thorns, thistles, and weeds will not have to be dealt with. There will be no poor. There will be plenty for everyone. The earth will be what God intended in the Garden of Eden. What an earth to live in! And there will be peace. Saints, we will have our new bodies and we will be reigning and ruling with King Jesus. I can't wait.

The land, when this earthquake takes place, is going to experience some major geographical changes. Perhaps, the most major change will be that it will create the "highest" mountain in the world. On these mountains will be located the millennial Jerusalem and the millennial temple. Millennial Jerusalem will be exalted above the hills. Jesus Christ will rule and reign from the millennial temple that will be located near the city. The prophet Micah does a good job of explaining this mountain. He says:[178]

"But in the latter days it shall come to pass, that the mountain of Jehovah's house shall be established on the top of the mountains, and it shall be exalted above the hills, and people shall flow into it. And many nations shall go and say, come ye and let us go to the mountain of Jehovah, and to the house of the God of Jacob; and he will teach us of his ways, and we will walk in his paths. For out of Zion shall go forth the law, and the word of Jehovah from Jerusalem.

People will flow into it and nations shall go to be taught his ways and the people will walk according to the way that they have been taught. This passage says the law shall go forth out of Zion. Nations will be required to come to Jerusalem. If they do not, they will be punished by the withholding of rain from their nation.

In Ezekiel, we find a description of this high mountain where the millennial Jerusalem and the millennial temple is located (Ezekiel, Chapters 40-48). This highest mountain is to be 50 miles square. It is divided into three sections:

1. The northern section which will be 20 miles by 50 miles. In the center of this section is where the millennial temple is located. The priests will occupy this section. The priests who will occupy this area are the descendants of Zadak. This is because these descendants of the Tribe of Levi remained faithful when others went astray.

2. The central section also is 20 miles by 50 miles. This central section will be assigned to the Tribe of Levi.

3. The southern section measure 10 miles by 50 miles. The millennial Jerusalem is to be located in the center of this section. The size of millennial Jerusalem will be 10 miles square. There will be two sections on either side of Jerusalem. An east and west, if you will. These two sections will be for growing of food for those who live and work in Jerusalem.

Jerusalem will be for all members of the Twelve Tribes of Israel. It does not have a particular assignment for the inhabitants. On each side of Jerusalem will be two large fields. Each will be 10 miles by 20 miles. Stop and think for a minute how large these fields will be. With the curse lifted and the rich soil without briars, thorns, and weeds, these two fields will produce a great amount of food. Saints stop and think how wonderful it is going to be to live in our new bodies during the millennium. And our home will be in the New Jerusalem.

C. The Millennial Temple

According to Ezekiel 37:26-28, God's sanctuary will be located in the midst of Israel. The temple will be larger than all previous temples. It will be about one mile square. Can you believe a temple will be one mile square? That is a large temple. In Ezekiel 43:1-9, we find the return of the Shechinah Glory. The Shechinah Glory is a "visible manifestation of the presence of God." [179] When the Babylonians destroyed the temple, the Shechinah Glory vanished. It has not returned until the building of the millennial temple. When it returns, it will never depart from Israel again. It will dwell in the midst of Israel forever. The millennial temple will be the center of Jewish and Gentile worship during the millennium. The millennial temple will not have the "Ark of the Covenant."

D. The Millennial River

God is so awesome and complete. Here, God sends water from this high mountain from the temple to places that need water and changes what needs changing like the Dead Sea. When this water flows into the Dead Sea, it will no longer be dead. This water will heal the Dead Sea and furnish it with fish. Ezekiel 47:8-10 says it will begin swarming with life. *"There shall be a very great multitude of fish."*…*"that fishers shall stand by it: from En-gedi even unto Eneglaim shall be a place for the spreading of nets; their fish shall be after their kinds, as the fish of the great sea, exceeding many."* [180] (See illustration Fruchtenbaum p. 465).

E. The Millennial Mountain

When Jesus Christ plants his feet on the Mount of Olives at his second coming, the greatest earthquake in all of history will take place. This earthquake will create major geographical and topographical change in Israel. One of the major changes this will create is the formation of the highest mountain in the world. Earthly Jerusalem as well as the millennial temple will be located on top of this very high mountain. Isaiah 2:2-4 sheds light on this great change and how this change effects our relationship to new earthly Jerusalem and with each other and with the nations of the earth. These are very powerful verses for those not only who will take up residence in the millennium but throughout the earth. Let's look at what the verses say: [181]

"And it shall come to pass in the latter days, that the mountain of Jehovah's house shall be established on the top of the mountain, and shall be exalted above the hills; and all nations shall flow into it. And many peoples shall go and say, come ye, and let us go up to the mountain of Jehovah, to the house of the God of Jacob; and he will teach us his ways, and we will walk in his paths; for out of Zion shall go forth the law, and the word of Jehovah from Jerusalem. And he will judge between the nations, and will decide concerning many peoples; and they shall beat their swords into plowshares, and their spears into pruning-hooks; nation shall not lift up sword against nation, neither shall they learn war anymore.

With the millennial kingdom, Israel will experience peace. Nations will be required to come to this new earthly Jerusalem in order to be taught the ways of God. If they do not, they will be punished by God by the withholding of rain. There will be peace because people will come to Jerusalem and they will be taught his ways. The laws will be planted in the hearts of people and they will obey the law. People will know they must go up to the mountain of Jehovah to learn the law. King Jesus resides in this temple atop this highest mountain. Plowshares and pruning-hooks may be needed. Swords and spears may not be needed. We will not have war anymore.

There has been war somewhere in the world just about all of my life. As I write this, I am trying to comprehend what living in this environment is going to be like. I'm ready to find out. Hallelujah!

F. Israel

For the first time in its history, Israel and the Jews will possess the Promised Land. Israel will be subdivided according to the twelve tribes. The northern tribes will include Dan, Asher, Naphlali, Manasseh, Ephraim, Reuben, and Judah. The southern tribes include Simeon, Issacher, Zebulum, Gad, and Benjamin (see illustration, p. 167). There is a large block of land that is assigned to the princes. It is labeled the Holy Oblation. It is a larger block of land than is assigned to the other tribes. Jerusalem is located in this portion of land. The land will reach well into Lebanon including most of that country and well past Damascus in Syria. The highest mountain where Jerusalem will be located is in this block of land. Jerusalem is located just west of the west bank.

The millennial Jerusalem will be 10 miles square. Each side will be 10 miles. Each side will have three gates. These gates will be named after the 12 sons of Jacob. On the north side will be Reuben, Judah, and Levi. On the east side, Joseph, Benjamin, and Dan. On the south side will be Simeon, Issachar, and Zebulum. On the west side will be Gad, Asher, and Naphtali. Jerusalem will have its name changed to Jehovah Shammah. The millennial Jerusalem will be so beautiful sitting upon the highest mountain in the world. We find in scripture that the millennial city will have several names. Some of the names include:

1. Jehovah Shammah (means Jehovah is there, Ezekiel 48:35)
2. The City of Peace

3. Jehovah our Righteousness (Jeremiah 33:16)
4. The City of God (Psalm 87:1-7)
5. The House of Jehovah (Psalm 122:1-9)
6. The Holy City

Whatever the name, that city will be so beautiful we cannot describe it. The Shechinah Glory will be everywhere you look. I believe that will even be the way we dress. Heaven's clothes will be beautiful.

There is a song that so many of us love. Its title, *Beulah Land*, is found in Isaiah 62:4. It is Isaiah's name for the Promised Land after the captivity. A symbol of Israel's future blessedness and prosperity. The title, *Beulah Land*, is found only one time in the bible.

I want to end this section by telling you I am reminded frequently to pray for Jerusalem. And I do. I end my prayer every night before I go to sleep by praying for Jerusalem. We are admonished in Psalm 122:6 to pray for the peace of Jerusalem. They shall prosper that love thee. I do not pray this prayer so that I will prosper. That will take care of itself. I pray this prayer because I want to be obedient to God. That is God's city. That is where he will rule and reign during the millennial kingdom. I teach my Wednesday night class to pray this prayer. Then extend it to include all of Israel. That is God's country. And then to include the Jews. They have been persecuted all across history. Learn to love the Jews. MY SAVIOR IS A JEW.

I also want to end this section of this writing by giving a great big footnote to Dr. Arnold Fruchtenbaum. Thank you, Dr. Fruchtenbaum.

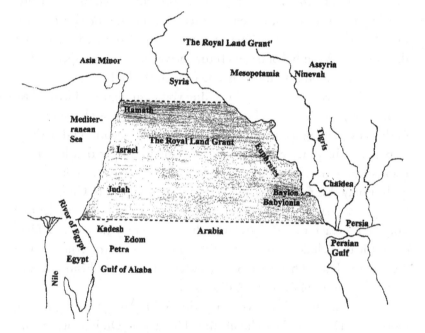

Illustration 2: The Royal Land Grant
Phillip Russell—A personal friend in the study of Bible prophecy.
(Permission granted)

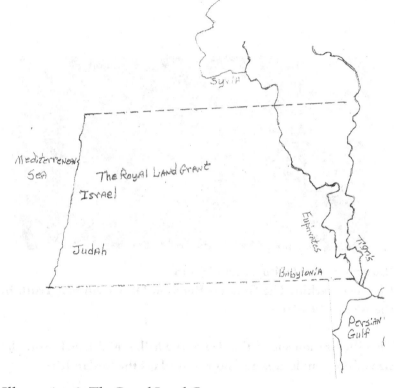

Illustration 3: The Royal Land Grant
Phillip Russell—A personal friend in the study of Bible prophecy.
(Permission granted)

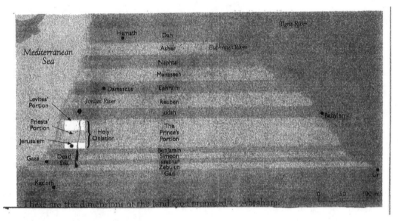

Illustration 4: The Royal Land Grant
Clarence Larkin, The Greatest Book on Dispensational Truth in the World, 1918, p. 94

This illustration shows the size of the Millennial Israel. Note the size of the temple area and how it overlaps the Jordan River.

THE TEMPLE

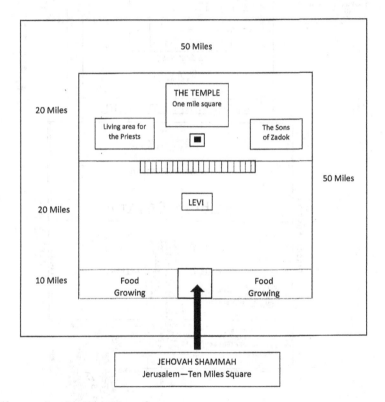

Illustration 5: The Temple
Dr. Arnold Fruchtenbaum, The Footsteps of the Messiah, Ariel Ministries, 2003, p. 450

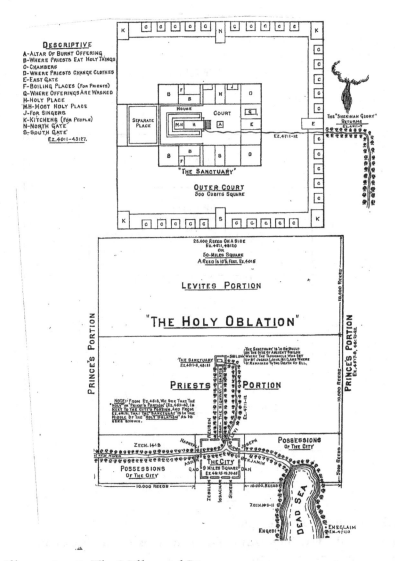

Illustration 9: The Millennial River
Clarence Larkin, The Greatest Book on Dispensational Truth in
the World, 1918, p. 94

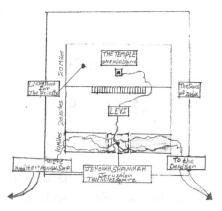

Illustration 10: The Millennial River
Dr. Arnold Fruchtenbaum, The Footsteps of the Messiah, Ariel
Ministries, 2003, p. 465

This drawing shows the origin of the water coming out from under
the sanctuary. It travels east for a short distance and then turns south
until it gets to the city. This is living water as we shall see. When the
river gets inside the city, the river forks. One part of the river turns
left going through the field that is east of the city and then it runs
into the Dead Sea. This water is fresh, clean, clear, and pure. It is
healing water. It turns the Dead Sea into a fresh water sea. It will not
be a salty water sea. This river will heal the Dead Sea. It will have
fish in it abundantly like the fish in the Great Sea (Mediterranean
Sea). Their fish shall be "according to their kind." According to the
fish of the Great Sea. The fish will be "exceeding many."

The other part of the fork turns right going through the field that
is west of the city. These two fields are for the production of food
for those working in the city. This part of the river after making
its way through the field west of the city makes its way to the
Mediterranean Sea.

163

Chapter 10

ANGELS

It becomes very obvious if you study the scriptures very long the significant role of angels in God's plan. Angels are created beings and were probably created the very first day the earth was created. We do not know how many angels God created. We just know there are a very large number of them. Jesus once said that He could call twelve legions of angels to protect Him. There are 6,000 angels in a legion. If He could call 12 legions that would equal 72,000 angels. That is a pretty large army of angels and that certainly would not be all of the angels. When Jesus returns to this earth at the Second Coming, He will bring with Him an army of angels. That army is referred to as a host of angels. We do not know how many that will be but we know it will be a very large number. In Revelation 19:14 it says:

"And the armies which were in heaven followed him upon white horses clothed in fine linen, white and clean."

Notice the word armies is plural. We can conclude that these armies will be a very large host of angels. I am looking forward to seeing the angels at work during the millennium. They will rule and reign with Jesus Christ and so will the saints. The angels will continue to do the bidding for the Lord Jesus Christ as He rules the earth during the millennium. We will then be able to see angels.

There are 66 books in the bible. Of the 66 books, 34 books make reference to angels. There are 300 references to angels in the bible. In Revelation 5:11, John saw ten thousand times ten thousand plus thousands of thousands of angels around God's throne in heaven. These numbers are plural and not singular. Trying to determine how many angels there are becomes an impossible task. Billy Graham in his book, *Angels: God's Secret Agents*, makes the statement that there are "millions of angels at God's command and at our service." Notice again the word millions is plural and not singular. This indicates that he believes there are a very large number of angels. Renald Showers in his book, *Angels*, says there is an indefinite number. There are hundreds and hundreds of millions, probably billions of angles. One writer believes that there are 2.1 million angels. I do not know how he arrived at that number but in any case there are a very, very large number of angels.

Angels don't die. They don't age. They don't marry. They cannot procreate and they are not omniscient. Angles are invisible and are spiritual beings. The scripture indicates that where angels do appear they are male. In the bible, angels are called "Sons of God." Most often they are between the ages of 24 and 41. Most angels do not have names; however, there are two angels that are mentioned in scripture by name. These are good angels and their names are Gabriel and Michael. Gabriel is a messenger and his role is to take messages for God to others. Michael is a warrior and his role is to serve as a protector of Israel.

Angels have a large number of varied activities. For example, look at all the information relative to the birth of Jesus. Gabriel brought the news to Mary that she would conceive and bear a son and she would name Him Jesus. Gabriel told Mary that she would conceive by the Holy Spirit and that she would bear a son and He would be the Messiah. Gabriel even told Mary what to name the child. We are reminded here of one of God's means that He used some two thousand years ago in His master plan with Mary and Joseph. It is interesting that God used an angel in His master plan. God spoke to Mary by using an angel and the angel told Mary that she was going to have a baby who would be the savior of the world. This was no ordinary experience for Mary. This was a very special, powerful, and significant experience from God. God was using these powerful experiences with an angel to get a job done. This was part of God's master plan.

Imagine how you would feel if you were a 15 or 16 year old virgin girl, and you received a message (from an angel) that you were going to have a baby. In this powerful and unique experience, the angel told you that this baby was going to be the savior of the world. Remember this is no ordinary experience. At 15 years of age, you do not understand all of this. Here God uses an angel to get His job done. This was part of His master plan.

Imagine also if you were Mary having to tell Joseph all that she had been told by this angel. Perhaps they go out on a date one night and Mary says to Joseph, "Joseph, there is something that I have to tell you...I'm pregnant." Joseph, startled at this confession, knows that he has never been with Mary. He says "you're what?" "I'm pregnant Joseph and please let me explain," replies Mary. Joseph, with every ounce of his being listens as Mary tells him about the powerful experience she had with the angel. Joseph loves Mary so much and he does not want her to be punished. Joseph is very troubled. God knows that He has another job to do. He now has to deal with Joseph. As Matthew 1:20 tells us, God also used an angel as a means to communicate with Joseph. He used this means for the solution to Joseph's struggle.

These had to be very powerful experiences with angels. They were no ordinary experiences. It is worthy to note that both Joseph and Mary did what God's plan had commanded of them. Mary risked everything to obey and be part of God's plan. Can you imagine how Mary felt when Joseph told her that he was not going to put her away? Joseph also obeyed God by taking Mary home to be his wife.

There are many, many other examples of how God used angels in all kinds of different ways. There are two others that I would like to include in this writing. Both are found in the book of Daniel. First, in the third chapter of the book of Daniel, three Jews, Shadrach, Meshach, and Abed-nego, refused to bow down and worship the golden image which King Nebuchadnezzar had set up. The punishment for this refusal would be that they would be thrown into a burning fiery furnace. These three Jews had jobs in the government of King Nebuchadnezzar. They were over the affairs of the province of Babylon. Certain Chaldeans told King Nebuchadnezzar that these three Jews were not worshipping the golden image that he had set up. King Nebuchadnezzar called them in and confronted them with this accusation. They answered and said the following to the king (Daniel 3:16-18):

> *O Nebuchadnezzar, we are not careful to answer thee in this matter. If it be so, our God whom we serve is able to deliver us from the burning fiery furnace, and he will deliver us out of thine hand, O King. But if not, be it known unto thee, O King, that we will not serve thy gods, nor worship the golden image which thou has set up.*

This made the king very angry. He commanded that they be bound and thrown into the burning fiery furnace that was seven times hotter than usual. The mighty men of the king's army bound them and threw them into the furnace. The furnace was so hot that the flame of the fire slew the men that put Shadrack, Meshack, and Abed-nego in the furnace.

> *…..Nebuchadnezzar said to his counselors, did we not cast three men bound into the midst of the fire…….Lo, I see four men loose, walking in the midst of the fire, and they have no hurt; and the form of the fourth is like the Son of God…..Then Shadrack, Meshach, and Abed-nego came fourth of the midst of the fire. And the princes, governors, and captains, and the king's counselors, being gathered together, saw these men, upon whose bodies the fire had not power, nor was a hair of their head singed, neither were their coats changed, nor the smell of fire has passed on them. Then Nebuchadnezzar spake, and said, blessed be the God of Shadrack, Meshack, and Abed-nego, who hath sent his angel and delivered his servants that trusted in him (Daniel 3:24-28).*

Here again, we see the work of one of God's angels in protecting the three Jews from the burning fiery furnace.

Daniel was thrown into the lion's den because of jealousy. King Darius could find no wrong in Daniel and he made him president over the whole kingdom. This angered others because they thought they were in line to get the job and be appointed president ahead of Daniel. These presidents and princes began trying to find a way to catch Daniel breaking some law. These governors, presidents, and princes consulted together to establish a royal statute that said "whosoever shall ask a petition of any God or man for thirty days," save the King, shall be cast into the den of lions. They were successful in getting the king to sign this decree. They knew that Daniel prayed three times a day. Daniel continued to pray. He opened his windows toward Jerusalem, he kneeled upon his knees three times a day and prayed, and he gave thanks before his God. These men found Daniel praying. They told King Darius that Daniel had broken the decree that he had signed. King Darius liked Daniel and he did not want to issue the punishment of casting Daniel into the den of lions but he did and he did not sleep any that night. King Darius even told Daniel that his God would deliver him. King Darius arose very early the next morning and went in hast unto the den of lions. When he arrived, he found Daniel unharmed. King Darius was glad. Daniel told the king the following:

> *My God hath sent his angel, and hath shut the lions mouths, that they have not hurt me.....Daniel was taken up out of the den, and no manner of hurt was found upon him, because he believed in his God. And the king commanded, and they brought those men which had accused Daniel, and they cast them into the den of lions, them, their children, and their wives; and the lions had the mastery of them, and brake all their bones in pieces or ever they came at the bottom of the den (Daniel 6:22, 24).*

Don't tell me there are not angels at work in this world.

Chapter 11

WAS HE AN ANGEL?

One weekend when I was singing with the Jericho Quartet, we had a date at a college in Oklahoma on Saturday night and then on Sunday afternoon the following day in Russellville, Arkansas. After our concert in Oklahoma, we found a motel and stayed there for the night. Our date in Russellville, Arkansas was canceled because of stormy weather and storm warnings. Sunday morning, we started home to Tuscumbia, Alabama. My car would just not run. I would go about one half mile or maybe a mile and it would start sputtering and missing and then would shut down. So we loaded all we could into one car including five members of the group and sent them home to Tuscumbia, Alabama. One member of that group was my son who would graduate from high school on Monday night so we had to get him home. I stayed with my car in Russellville, Arkansas to get it repaired first thing Monday morning and then I would drive home and be there for the graduation. You just don't miss your son's high school graduation.

They worked on my car first thing Monday morning and announced that it was ready to go. I paid the man and headed for home. About 10 or 15 miles down the interstate the car began to sputter and miss just like before. I looked to my right and saw a Texaco station and there was a mechanic on duty. I explained my situation and he believed he could fix it quickly. So very shortly I backed out and started up the ramp to the interstate. About halfway up the ramp to the interstate the car shut down. I eased the car to the edge of the pavement and put my head down on the steering wheel and prayed, "Lord, what can I do?"

At that point, a car pulled up right beside me. I was frightened. I rolled my window down and he rolled his window down. There were two other men in the car other than the driver. The driver looked at me and said "Sir, you have problems, don't you?" With tears in my eyes and in a low voice, I answered "yes." He said, "may I help you?" I asked him if there was a rent- a-car nearby. He said "yes, about ten miles out at the airport." I asked him if he would lead me to the airport and he said he would. I told him if I started lagging behind to stop because my car was about to shut down. For 10 miles I would go about one half mile and my car would be just about ready to shut down. I would start it again and go as fast as I could and it would shut down. I would let it coast for as long as I could. Then I would start it again and get all I could from this start and go. We finally made it to the airport and the man led me inside to the counter where you could rent a car. He told the lady "this man needs a car." I had to fill out a form with a little information and then I gave it back to the lady. She said "the car is on its way to the front now." I was going to thank the man for his help and when I turned around he was gone. I had already asked him for his business card and he had given me one. I looked out front to see if he was at his car. There was no car. I was quite baffled. The rent a car came and I headed home.

All the way home, I wondered about what happened to that man. I remembered that I did get his business card before we talked to the lady at the counter. I drove home from Russellville, Arkansas and broke every speed limit in Arkansas, Tennessee, Alabama, and Mississippi, but I got home in time for my son's high school graduation. As I pulled into the driveway at home, the family was dressed ready to go to the graduation. I changed clothes and went with them.

The next week I wrote the man a letter. I told him all that I had gone through and thanked him for his help. Without his help, I would have missed my son's graduation from high school. I mailed the letter using the address that was on the card that he gave me. A few days later, I received the letter in the mail with a stamp on it. It said "no such address in Russellville, Arkansas, and no name is listed in our mailing list." I called information to see if there was a telephone number by that name. They checked and found no such name. They told me that no such name could be found.

Was this man an angel sent by God to help me when I needed help? It is not always safe on interstate highways. Then a strange car drives up beside you and the individual inside asks if you need any help. I was frightened and scared. The men in the car were in their 30's. There were three of them and there was only one of me. I was a long way from home. They had a car that would run. I didn't. I have always believed that man was an angel sent by God to help me. You see, I needed to get home and I didn't have much time left to get to my son's graduation. God is always just in time.

I do not know where that car came from when I was sitting on the edge of the pavement in Russellville, Arkansas. I do not know what happened to that man when I turned around to thank him at that rent-a-car counter. He was gone and so was his car. I tried to find the man and was unable to find him. I believed that he was an angel sent by God to help me. I still do.

I told the lady at the counter that I would be back in a few days to get my car. She told me that they would put it in a shop just across the street and they would repair the car.

In a few days, my brother and I went to Russellville, Arkansas to get my car. It ran fine until just east of Corinth, Mississippi, and it stopped again. I pulled off the highway and left the car there on the side of the road. The next day my brother and I went to get the car with his truck. We carried a chain and we were going to pull it home. When we got to the car I suggested that I might see if it would start. It did and I told him to follow me to see how far I could get. I made it all the way home (about 40 miles). Needless to say, I traded for another car.

I believe I had an experience with an angel. There were just too many things that were unexplainable. I hope when I get to heaven that he will walk up to me and say, I was the angel that helped you in Russellville, Arkansas. Remember!

ENDNOTES

1   J. Vernon McGee, *Thru the Bible*, 1982, Thomas Nelson, Inc., p. 587.
2   Daniel's Seventy Weeks of Years, 2011, The Olive Press, p. 11.
3   J. Vernon McGee, *Thru the Bible*, 1982, Thomas Nelson, Inc., p. 587.
4   Dr. Arnold G. Fruchtenbaum, *The Footsteps of the Messiah*, Ariel Ministries, 2004, p. 191.
5   Ibid, p. 192.
6   Alva McCain, *Daniel's Prophecy of the 70 Weeks*, 2007, BMH Books, p. 12-13.
    1. Dr. Arnold G. Fruchtenbaum, *The Footsteps of the Messiah*, Ariel Ministries, 2004, p.66.
    2. Revelation 2:7, 11, 17, 29; 3:6,13,22.
7   G. H. Pember, *Great Prophecies of the Bible*, 4 Vols. Reprinted, Miami Springs, FL: Conely and Schoettle Publishers, 1984, p. 497.
8   Dr. Arnold G. Fruchtenbaum, *The Footsteps of the Messiah: A Study of the Sequence of Prophetic Events*, Tustin, CA: Ariel Press, 1982, p.36.
9   Thomas Ice and Timothy Demy, *Fast Facts on Bible Prophecy*, Harvest House Publishers, 1977, p. 46.
10 Ibid.
11 J. Vernon McGee, *Thru the Bible*, Thomas Nelson Publishers, 1983, p. 470.
12 J. Dwight Pentecost, *Things to Come*, Zondervan, 1964, p.155.
13 2 Peter 3:8
14 Jude 14 and 15.
15 Randy Alcorn, *Heaven*, Tyndale House Publishing, Inc., 2004, p. 280.
16 Ibid, p. 288.
17 Hank Hanegroaff
18 Ibid. p.289
19 Ibid, p.289

20 John Hagee, *His Glory Revealed*, Thomas Nelson Publishers, 1999, p. 64.

21 Psalm 139:14.

22 John Walvoord

23 Randy Alcorn, *Heaven*, Tyndale House Publishing, Inc., 2004, p. 117.

24 Revelation 7:9.

25 Ibid. p.7:10-13.

26 Ibid.

27 Ibid. p. 7:9.

28 Ibid. p. 7:10-12.

29 Ibid.

30 Ibid. p. 19:8.

31 Ibid.

32 Ibid. p. 6:9-11.

33 II Corinthians 5:8.

34 Revelation 20:4.

35 Ibid. p. 19:14.

36 Ibid. p. 3:5.

37 Ibid. p. 3:18.

38 Acts 1:9-11.

39 Webster's Dictionary

40 *Maranatha: Our Lord Come! A Definitive Study of the Rapture of the Church*; Bellmauer, NJ: The Friends of Israel Gospel Ministry, Inc., 1995, p. 243.

41 Revelation 3:10.

42 1 Thessalonians 1:10.

43 Ibid. p. 5:9.

44 *Encyclopedia of Bible Prophecy*, Edited by Tim LaHaye and Ed Hindson, Harvest House Publishers, 2004, p. 225).

45 Mark Hitchcock, *The End*, Tyndale House Publishers, 2012, pp 137-138.

46 J. Dwight Pentecost, *Things to Come,* Zonderrean, 1964, pp. 158-161.

47 Ibid, pp. 161-163.

48 Acts 2.

49 1 Thessalonians 4:13-18.

50 Hebrews 9:27.

51 John 14:1-3.

52 Ibid. p. 14:9.

53 John Walvoord, *Prophecy in the New Millennium,* Kregel Publications, 2001, p. 18.

54 Revelation 20:4-6.

55 J. Dwight Pentecost, *Things to Come*, Zondervan, 1958, p. 576.

56 Hebrews 11:5

57 Webster's Dictionary.

58 Luke 21:36.

59 1 Thessalonians 1:10.

60 Revelation 3:10.

61 1 Thessalonians 5:9.

62 Romans 5:9.

63 John 14:3.

64 John Hagee, *From Daniel to Doomsday*, Thomas Nelson, Inc. 1979, p. 114.

65 II Peter 3:3-4.

66 John 14-2-3.

67 Psalm 83:4.

68 John 14:2-3.

69 Ibid. p. 14:9.

70 Matthew 25:21.

71 Mark Hitchcock, *The End*, Tyndale Publishing, 2012, p. 211.

72 Revelation 4:9-11.

73 Ibid. p.7:10-11.

74 1 Corinthians 13:12.

75 Randy Alcorn, Tyndale, 2004, p. 215.

76 Luke 14:11.

77 Revelation, Chapter 19:7-9.

78 Ibid. p. 19:9.

79 Ibid.

80 Grant R. Jeffrey, *Apocalypse: The Coming Judgment of the Nations*, Bantam Books, 1994, p. 237.

81 Ibid.

82 2 Corinthians 5:8.

83 I Corinthians 13:12.

84 Matthew 24:5-11.

85 Ibid. p. 37.

86 Genesis 6:11.

87 Hosea 6:1-3.

88 Romans 11:25-27.

89 Isaiah 53:1-9.

90 Ibid. p. 34:1-7.

91 Ibid. p. 63:1-6.

[92]   Habakkuk 3:3.

[93]   Micah 2:12-13.

[94]   Matthew 24:29-30.

[95]   Revelation 19:11-16.

[96]   Acts 1:9-11.

[97]   Matthew 16:27.

[98]   Micah 2:12-13.

[99]   Isaiah 34: 1-7.

[100] Ibid. p. 63:1-4.

[101] Ibid. p. 63:1.

[102] Zechariah 12:8-9.

[103] Ibid. p. 14:4.

[104] Revelation 16:17-21.

[105] Ibid.

[106] Ibid.

[107] Ibid.

[108] Dr. Arnold Fruchtenbaum, *The Footsteps of the Messiah*, p. 365.

[109] Tim LaHaye and Ed Hindson, *The Popular Encyclopedia of Bible Prophecy*, Harvest House Publishers, p. 175.

[110] Ibid.

[111] Genesis 12:3.

[112] Amos 9:14-15.

[113] Tim LaHaye and Ed Hindson, *The Popular Encyclopedia of Bible Prophecy*, Harvest House Publishers, p. 176.

[114] Ibid.

[115] Dr. Arnold Fruchtenbaum, *The Footsteps of the Messiah*, p. 369.

[116] Daniel 12:2.

[117] Revelation 20:4.

[118] Ibid. p. 20:11-15.

[119] Mark Hitchcock, *The End*, Tyndale Publishing, 2012, p. 394-395.

[120] Ephesians 4:11.

[121] Ibid.

[122] Mark Hitchcock.

[123] Ibid.

[124] Randy Alcorn, *Heaven*, Tyndale House Publishing, Inc., 2004, p. 211.

[125] Daniel 7:14-22.

[126] Ephesians 4:1.

[127] Dr. Arnold Fruchtenbaum, *The Footsteps of the Messiah*, p. 407.

[128] Ibid.

[129] Isaiah 9:6.
[130] Ibid. p. 16:5.
[131] Luke 1:33.
[132] Psalm 2:9.
[133] Ezekiel 34:23-24.
[134] Isaiah 32:1.
[135] Rosenbery, *Epicenter*, Tyndale, 2006, pg. 86.
[136] Psalm 8.
[137] Walvoord, 1999, p. 195.
[138] Ezekiel 39:4.
[139] Isaiah 17:1.
[140] Hagee, 2006, p. 105.
[141] Ezekiel 38:4.
[142] Ibid. p. 39:17-22.
[143] Genesis 12:3.
[144] Amos 9:14-15.
[145] Ezekiel 38: 9-10.
[146] Ibid. p. 38:9, 15, 16.
[147] Revelation 3:10.
[148] 1 Thessalonians 1:10.
[149] Ibid. p. 5:9.
[150] Romans 5:9.
[151] Luke 21:36.
[152] John Walvoord, *Prophecy in the New Millennium*, 2001, p. 122.
[153] John Walvoord, *The Nations in Prophecy*, Zondervan, p. 105.
[154] Psalm 83:3-5.
[155] Isaiah 17:1.
[156] Amos 9:14-15.
[157] Luke 21:28.
[158] II Chronicles 7:14.
[159] Dr. Arnold G. Fruchtenbaum, *The Footsteps of the Messiah*, Ariel Ministries 2003.
[160] Ibid. p. 384.
[161] Ibid. p. 377.
[162] Jeremiah 31:31-34.
[163] Dr. Arnold G. Fruchtenbaum, *The Footsteps of the Messiah*, Ariel Ministries, 2003, p. 405.
[164] Ibid.
[165] Hosea 6:1-3.

[166] Dr. Arnold G. Fruchtenbaum, *The Footsteps of the Messiah*, Ariel Ministries, 2003, p. 411.

[167] Ibid. p. 414.

[168] Jeremiah 16:15.

[169] Ezekiel 11:14-18.

[170] Amos 9:14-15.

[171] Dr. Arnold G. Fruchtenbaum, *The Footsteps of the Messiah*, Ariel Ministries, 2003, p. 419.

[172] Matthew 24:31.

[173] Genesis 13:14-17.

[174] 2 Samuel 7.

[175] Psalm 89:29.

[176] Ibid. p.89:34-37.

[177] Luke 1:32-33.

[178] Micah 4:1-2.

[179] *New Illustrated Bible Dictionary*, Thomas Nelson Publishers, 1986, p.1161.

[180] Ezekiel 47:8-10.

[181] Isaiah 2:2-4.

Printed in the United States
By Bookmasters